SALMON

SWIMMING FOR SURVIVAL

ROWENA RAE

ORCA BOOK PUBLISHERS

Published in Canada and the United States
in 2022 by Orca Book Publishers.
orcabook.com

Library and Archives Canada Cataloguing in Publication
Title: Salmon : swimming for survival / Rowena Rae.
Names: Rae, Rowena, author.
Series: Orca wild.
Description: Series statement: Orca wild |
Includes bibliographical references and index.
Identifiers: Canadiana (print) 20210179635 |
Canadiana (ebook) 20210179651 | ISBN 9781459826533 (hardcover) |
ISBN 9781459826540 (PDF) | ISBN 9781459826557 (EPUB)
Subjects: LCSH: Salmon—Juvenile literature.
Classification: LCC QL638.S2 R34 2022 | DDC j597.5/6—dc23)

Library of Congress Control Number: 2021934729

Summary: Part of the Orca Wild series, this nonfiction
book for middle-grade readers explores the iconic life cycle
of salmon, their contributions to the ecosystem and their
struggle for survival. Illustrated with photos throughout.

Orca Book Publishers is committed to reducing
the consumption of nonrenewable resources in the
making of our books. We make every effort to use
materials that support a sustainable future.

Orca Book Publishers gratefully acknowledges the support
for its publishing programs provided by the following
agencies: the Government of Canada, the Canada Council
for the Arts and the Province of British Columbia through
the BC Arts Council and the Book Publishing Tax Credit.

Front and back cover photos by DaveAlan/
Getty Images and Westend61/Getty Images
Design by Dahlia Yuen
Edited by Kirstie Hudson

Printed and bound in South Korea.

25 24 23 22 • 1 2 3 4

Kokanee salmon swim up Taylor Creek in California to spawn. Kokanee
are a freshwater variant of the oceangoing sockeye salmon.
VICKI JAURON, BABYLON AND BEYOND PHOTOGRAPHY/GETTY IMAGES

For my mother, who gave me my love of books and reading.

CONTENTS

Me on the right with my brother-in-law, Matt, in dry suits, ready to start snorkeling on the Stellako River, BC. Behind us is François Lake.
ANDREW WILSON

INTRODUCTION
SWIMMING WITH SALMON

My neck hurt from craning to look forward. My fingers ached from the cold water. My left knee throbbed from slamming into a boulder. But I didn't mind any of this. I was floating down a river with fish, each one about the length of my arm, swimming toward me.

The fish were sockeye salmon. As they swam, their cherry-red bodies undulated and their olive-green heads nodded ever so slightly.

These salmon were taking the second river journey of their lives. The first had been as young fish, traveling downstream on their way to the ocean. Now, as mature adults, they were returning. They had swum more than 500 miles (805 kilometers) from the Pacific Ocean up the Fraser River to their birthplace, the Stellako River. They had swum all this way—against the current—to create the next generation of salmon.

A male sockeye salmon swims upstream in his spawning colors in the Adams River, BC.
DARRYL LENIUK/GETTY IMAGES

I was floating down this river with three friends, one of them a fish biologist. Two river bends and hundreds more salmon later, we hauled ourselves onto the riverbank. I yanked the mask and snorkel from my face and caught the stench of two salmon carcasses rotting beneath a huckleberry bush. I wrinkled my nose. This was the smell of death—and also of rebirth.

Those fish would decay and eventually become basic nutrients dissolved in the river water. The nutrients would be sucked from the water by *algae*, *aquatic* organisms similar to plants, which grow like furry carpets over the rocks on the riverbed. The algae would be grazed by insect *larvae*, and the next spring, those insects would become food for juvenile, or young, salmon. The juvenile salmon would begin the circle of life anew.

In this book, I'm going to take you into the salmon's world. It's a complex world, involving fresh water and seawater. It's a dangerous world, with *predators* and high dams, fishing nets and changing ocean conditions. And it's an inspiring world, with a fish that keeps coming back to its birthplace, keeps swimming upstream, keeps fighting for the next generation.

Grab a mask and snorkel, and let's dive into the salmon's watery world!

A sockeye salmon decaying in the shallows of a river after spawning.
JEFF FOOTT/GETTY IMAGES

Atlantic salmon migrating through the ocean.
NICK HAWKINS

A female pink salmon eyes the photographer.
EIKO JONES

1

MEET THE
SALMON

Have you met the Salmonidae family? It's quite a large family, with relatives spread through much of the northern hemisphere. Some of them now live in the south too—Chile, New Zealand and Australia—because people took them there. But their true home is the north, in rivers, streams and sometimes lakes, and in the oceans— the North Pacific and the North Atlantic.

As with most families, the Salmonidae share some characteristics—fins, scales, large eyes, sensitive noses, *carnivorous* feeding habits and a need for cool, clear, fast-moving streams. Most, though not all, Salmonidae also migrate to the open ocean to grow up. Later in life, when they're mature, they return to their birthplace to start the next generation. The parents of many Salmonidae die within hours or days of *spawning* this new generation. Others turn tail and return to the ocean to live longer and spawn again.

The Salmonidae family includes the salmon and their cousins, the trout, char and grayling. In this book, I focus on salmon, which have captured people's hearts and filled their bellies for thousands of years.

The Yukon River starts in Northern British Columbia and flows north through Yukon. It eventually turns west and flows through Alaska, finally emptying into the Bering Sea.
MARK NEWMAN/GETTY IMAGES

SALMON COUNTRY

The Salmonidae family of fish is old—around 100 million years old—so some salmon ancestors lived at the same time as dinosaurs. The salmon we know today have a *common ancestor*. Around 15 to 20 million years ago, this common ancestor evolved into the two groups we call Atlantic salmon and Pacific salmon.

Atlantic salmon are native to *ecosystems* in both Europe and North America. Their historical range went from Portugal and Spain in the south to the White Sea in northwestern Russia. The countries of northwest Europe, the Baltic Sea, Britain and Ireland, and Iceland all had wild Atlantic salmon. On the other side of the Atlantic Ocean, their range went from Long Island Sound in New York north along the New England states and throughout Canada's Maritime provinces, parts of Quebec, and Newfoundland and Labrador. Today, Atlantic salmon still live in some of these places, but in others they no longer exist.

The range of Pacific salmon extends along western North America, from Northern California to Alaska and into the Beaufort Sea. On the other side of the Pacific Ocean, they are found in Japan, North Korea, South Korea, eastern China and Siberia (northern Russia). Today, Pacific salmon still live in these places, although in many areas they are struggling to survive.

Opposite:

Top: The pink line shows the approximate boundaries of wild Atlantic salmon in the ocean and on land today. The dots show places with rivers and streams that Atlantic salmon used to migrate to, but they don't any more. ADAPTED FROM FREE VECTOR MAPS

Bottom: The yellow line shows the boundaries for wild Pacific salmon in the ocean and on land. The line over the land is quite wiggly because it marks the shape of the watersheds where salmon rivers flow. WILD SALMON CENTER

Iceland

White Sea

Newfoundland
and Labrador

Baltic Sea

United
Kingdom

Quebec

Ireland

Russia

NORTH
ATLANTIC

Portugal

Long Island
Sound

Spain

— Existing
⣿ Extinct

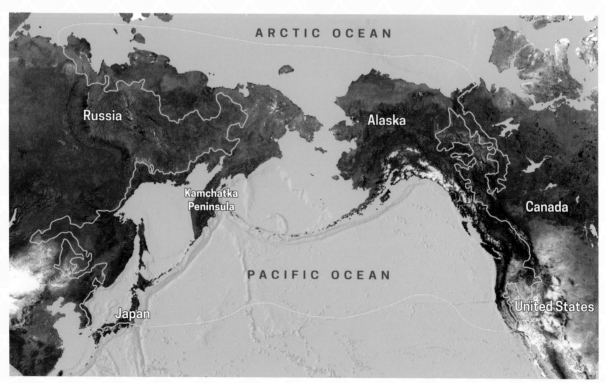

ARCTIC OCEAN

Russia

Alaska

Kamchatka
Peninsula

Canada

PACIFIC OCEAN

Japan

United States

Alanna Syliboy and her baby, Sage, release an adult Atlantic salmon into the Stewiacke River near their home community of Sipekne'katik in Nova Scotia.
ALANNA SYLIBOY

JUMPING IN

Alanna Syliboy's work with the Confederacy of Mainland Mi'kmaq Tribal Council takes her out to the rivers and into the Mi'kmaw communities around mainland Nova Scotia. Alanna uses Two-Eyed Seeing, which means looking at an issue from different perspectives—literally observing with two eyes, one open to Indigenous knowledge and the other open to Western knowledge. The idea is to bring together the view from both eyes to help solve shared problems. Alanna also speaks with Elders and other knowledge holders in her own community of Sipekne'katik First Nation and other Mi'kmaw communities to collect and record their knowledge about salmon and aquatic ecosystems. All of this work builds toward one thing: helping Plamu, the Atlantic salmon.

> "WHAT I DO TODAY IS GOING TO AFFECT WHAT HAPPENS TOMORROW."
> —ALANNA SYLIBOY

NAME-DROPPING

Atlantic salmon are in a *genus*, or group, called *Salmo*, and Pacific salmon are in a genus with a nearly unpronounceable name—*Oncorhynchus* (pronounced with the stress on the syllable in capital letters: on-KOR-in-kiss).

The *Salmo* genus contains many different species of trout and just one species of salmon, the Atlantic salmon. The scientific name of an Atlantic salmon is *Salmo salar*. The species name comes from the Latin word *salire*, which means "leap" or "jump." This refers to salmon's amazing ability to jump up and over waterfalls as they swim upstream as adult fish. Some of them can leap as high as 12 feet (3.7 meters) to get over obstacles. That's like you—if you're about four and a half feet (1.4 meters) tall—leaping up from the pool deck and over the 16-foot (4.9-meter) diving platform!

The *Oncorhynchus* genus contains a few species of trout and six species of Pacific salmon. The genus name comes from two Greek words. The word *onkos* means "hook," and *rynchos* means "nose." Fish in this genus, especially the males, develop a hook-shaped nose when they come back to rivers as adults. Here are the six Pacific salmon species (*O.* stands for *Oncorhynchus*):

1. Chinook or king salmon, *O. tshawytscha* (sha-WEET-sha)

2. Chum salmon, *O. keta* (KEY-ta)

3. Coho salmon, *O. kisutch* (KI-such)

4. Pink salmon, *O. gorbuscha* (gor-BOO-sha)

5. Sockeye salmon, *O. nerka* (NER-ka)

6. Masu or cherry salmon, *O. masou* (ma-SOO)

Coho salmon spawn in a shallow river. The male fish (left) has bright spawning colors and a very hooked nose. The female fish (right) has more subdued colors.
EIKO JONES

The spots on this juvenile Atlantic salmon help to camouflage it among the rocks of a riverbed.
NICK HAWKINS

THE BEST OF BOTH WORLDS

Atlantic and Pacific salmon share the ability to split their lives between two exceptionally different environments, fresh water and salt water. Science has a term to describe this lifestyle: *anadromy*. Anadromous fish hatch from an egg in fresh water, spend some of their youth in streams or lakes, then migrate to the ocean to grow into mature fish. When they are fully grown, they swim back to their birth river and go upstream all the way to where they hatched. There the fish spawn—female fish lay eggs, and male fish fertilize them.

The switch from fresh water to salt water is no easy feat for juvenile (young) salmon. It requires changes inside and outside their bodies—more on these changes in chapter 2. After living in the ocean for two to five years (depending on the species and ocean conditions), the large, silvery adult fish reverse their internal changes so they can once again survive in fresh water. They also change their outer color and shape to attract mates when they finally reach the place where they'll spawn.

Why go through all these dramatic changes to travel between fresh water and salt water and back again?

It takes a lot of energy and time to do this, so why not just stay in one place?

Anadromy evolved as a way to take advantage of the best of both worlds. Rivers and streams have safer places for eggs to incubate and for small fish to enter the world. There are more places to hide from predators. There's food, too, but not tons of it. That's where the ocean comes in. The sea is teeming with *zooplankton*—tiny animals such as copepods, amphipods and krill, which are suspended in the water. Salmon chow down on the zooplankton and later they also eat small fish like capelin and herring. By gorging on the smorgasbord available in the ocean, salmon can grow big quickly, and the females can produce lots of eggs.

JUMPING IN

Dylan Parliament has loved fish for as long as he can remember. When he was three years old, he memorized the names of fish in guidebooks. When he was six, he caught his first fish—a bass—in an Ontario lake. He was hooked! Dylan began helping the North Shore Streamkeepers with fish surveys and other work on Hastings Creek, which runs through North Vancouver, BC. A few years later, his family decided to move to a new home. The first place they looked at had Hastings Creek running right through the property!

Today Dylan still surveys the fish in the creek—simply by taking his nets out the back door. "His" creek is shaded by trees and has cutthroat trout and crayfish in it. In the fall, coho salmon and steelhead rainbow trout swim upstream to spawn. "I love all the wildlife on my doorstep," Dylan says. "It's cool to go out and see everything."

"UNDERSTAND [SALMON'S] HABITAT AS THEIR OWN WORLD AND TRY TO PROTECT THAT."
—DYLAN PARLIAMENT

Dylan Parliament measures the length of a juvenile cutthroat trout. This species, *Oncorhynchus clarkii*, is classified in the same genus as the Pacific salmon.
MARIA HUDSPITH AND DEB PARLIAMENT

WILD ATLANTIC SALMON
a wondrous life cycle

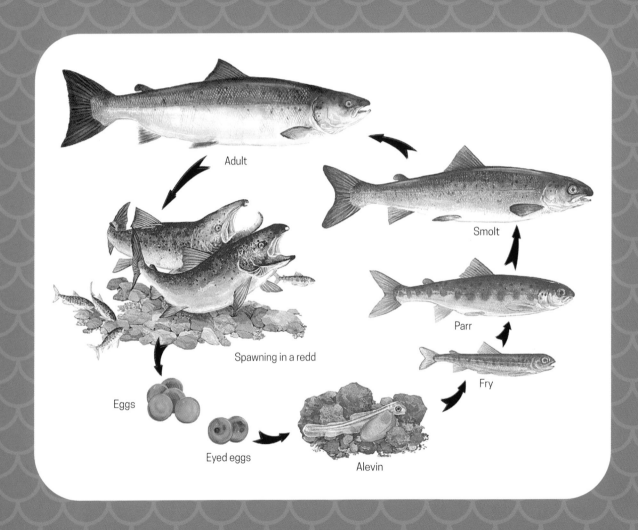

Adult

Spawning in a redd

Smolt

Parr

Fry

Eggs

Eyed eggs

Alevin

This illustration shows the life cycle of Atlantic salmon, but all species of salmon have the same basic life cycle.

2

THE CYCLE OF LIFE

Nature loves cycles—things going from one stage or phase to another, and then another, and another. You probably already have an idea of the salmon's life cycle. Atlantic and Pacific salmon have a similar cycle with a series of basic stages.

THROUGH THE AGES

PERFECT PACKAGE: THE EGG

Each female fish lays thousands of eggs in a gravel nest, called a *redd*. Male fish fertilize the eggs with their sperm, called *milt*. Fertilized eggs lie in the spaces between pieces of gravel and incubate for six weeks to five months (the length of time depends on the species and water temperature).

Inside the egg, an embryo is growing and feeding on the egg yolk. Eggs are delicate and need clean gravel with lots of oxygen-rich water flowing around them. If silt or other muck gets dumped on the gravel, it smothers and kills the eggs.

Eggs laid by Atlantic salmon nestle in the gravel of a streambed. Each egg is about the size of a new eraser on the end of a pencil.
NICK HAWKINS

A group of salmon alevins. Each one is about the length of a standard paper clip.
EIKO JONES

ALIEN BEING: THE ALEVIN

When the embryo is ready to hatch, it breaks free of its eggshell and stays hidden in the gravel as a strange-looking creature. An *alevin* looks a bit like a piece of yarn with eyes at one end and a distorted, orangish marble attached to its belly. The ungainly marble is the yolk sac, which continues to nourish the little fish for weeks or even months. Once it has used up and absorbed its yolk sac, the alevin swims up through the gravel.

LITTLE-KID FISH: THE FRY

Now a little fish about 1 inch (2.5 centimeters) long, the *fry* is ready to start eating insect larvae, adult insects and other *invertebrates* that live in or fall into the water.

Fry are tasty snacks for bigger fish, snakes, birds and even some stream invertebrates like dragonfly larvae. So fry hide in dark pools underneath fallen logs and behind rocks, and in nooks and crannies along the edges of rivers. These nooks and crannies are more properly called *side channels*—places like *sloughs*, ponds, marshes and *oxbows*—and they're critical *habitat* for salmon fry and other small fish.

Salmon fry behave in a few different ways, depending on their species. Sockeye fry swim to a lake, while pink and chum fry go straight out to the ocean. These three species pretty much skip the next stage.

TWEEN FISH: THE PARR

Atlantic, chinook, coho and masu salmon fry all stay for a while in rivers and side channels, and they go through a tween stage in which they are called *parr*. They develop spots or stripes on their sides to camouflage themselves on the streambeds and help them avoid predators.

Some male Atlantic salmon parr postpone the next stage—going out to sea—and mature in the river. Then they swim to a spawning area and sneak in to fertilize a female's eggs when larger males aren't looking. This behavior gets them the label "precocious parr."

Beware! This salmon fry is looking for a meal.
EIKO JONES

An adult male Atlantic salmon protects his nest from precocious parr—the smaller fish milling around in the foreground.
NICK HAWKINS

TEENAGE FISH: THE SMOLT

Young salmon ready to go to sea enter the teenage stage. Called *smolts*, they make internal changes to keep the right balance of salts inside and outside their cells as they swim from fresh water through an *estuary* and into salt water. On the outside, their scales turn silver to make the fish less visible to ocean predators, and their shape becomes tapered at each end—like a torpedo—to help them with long-distance swimming. Smolts also group together in schools, to decrease the chance of being eaten by a predator. Safety in numbers!

By the time they enter the ocean, smolts are anywhere from 2 to 10 inches (5 to 25 centimeters) long, depending on the species. They are fully transformed and ready to grow big. Once at sea, they eat and eat and eat—the quicker they grow, the more likely they'll survive.

Salmon smolts swim through the estuary of the Naknek River, AK, on their way out to the open ocean.
NATALIE FOBES/GETTY IMAGES

Adult Atlantic salmon.
WESTEND61/GETTY IMAGES

SILVERY AND SLEEK: THE ADULT

Once in the ocean, salmon swim for thousands of miles in search of food. By the time they're mature, adult salmon measure 18 to 60 inches (46 to 152 centimeters) in length and weigh 3.5 to 50 pounds (1.6 to 23 kilograms), depending again on species. A few grow even bigger, weighing more than 100 pounds (45 kilograms)!

GREAT MIGRATOR: THE SPAWNER

After 18 months to 8 years in the ocean (depending on species), mature salmon act on the instinct to swim back to their birth streams. All salmon in the ocean are bright silver, but when they return to fresh water, they change color again, this time to combinations of brown, purplish, red and green, to attract a mate. Their bodies change shape—they may get a hooked nose, longer teeth or a humped back, depending on species and whether they're

GO WILD

Scientists think adult salmon use several tools to find their birth stream. First, they navigate by Earth's *magnetic field*, using it like a compass to cross the ocean. Other clues may also help them, such as day length, water salinity and temperature. They also use their birth river's chemical "smell," which they memorized as juveniles before going to sea. Biologists call this ability *imprinting*—a learning process in an animal's early life that affects its later behavior.

GO WILD

On the way to their birth river, a few salmon wander off course and enter other rivers. These straying fish are one of the reasons salmon have successfully populated so many rivers and streams. And they can be the secret to a *population's* survival if a catastrophe happens, like a landslide blocking a river.

Mount St. Helens in Washington State erupted in 1980, sending mudflows and hot water into the Toutle River. Later that year, oceangoing trout (relatives of salmon) that came back to spawn couldn't swim back up the destroyed Toutle River. Some of these fish strayed into other nearby rivers and kept the population alive.

male or female. Atlantic salmon males get a hooked lower jaw called a *kype*.

When they re-enter fresh water, salmon stop eating and live off their body fat as they swim upriver for hundreds of miles—in some cases, more than 1,000 miles (1,609 kilometers). When they finally reach the stretch of stream where they hatched, females use their remaining energy to build redds in the gravel and lay their eggs. A male sprays his milt over the redd to fertilize the eggs, and the female then covers the eggs with gravel using her strong tail. Females usually build and lay eggs in several redds. Males use some of their last energy to fight with other males for the right to fertilize a particular female's eggs. Males keep spawning with other females until they are worn out.

Atlantic salmon can survive after spawning and go on to spawn again in future years. The record for a single Atlantic salmon is spawning seven times in its life! An Atlantic salmon that has spawned is called a *kelt*. Kelts can hang out in the river, not eating, for months before going back out to sea. By comparison, the six species of Pacific salmon die within hours or days of spawning.

Male pink salmon get a humped back at spawning time, earning them the nicknames Humpback and Humpy.
EIKO JONES

Wooden salmon swim on a schoolyard fence behind Louise Towell. "I now meet people who are adults," she says, "and they remember being a kid and painting a fish."
PAUL CIPYWNYK

"KIDS KNOW THEY'RE HELPING THEIR COMMUNITY. THEY'RE HELPING SPREAD THE MESSAGE THAT WHATEVER WE DO ON LAND AFFECTS THE RIVERS, THE OCEAN, THE SALMON."
—LOUISE TOWELL

JUMPING IN

In British Columbia it's common to see wooden salmon swimming along schoolyard fences. Painted with stripes, spots, flowers or hearts, fish of every color twist left and right or curve in loops. These fish are part of a mural project that Louise Towell and her nine-year-old daughter, Chanel, dreamed up.

It started with an empty city lot surrounded by a chain-link fence. Louise and Chanel wanted to make it look better—less gray and desolate—but they weren't sure how. The answer came when someone poured a toxic substance down a storm drain that led to the local stream, killing many organisms, including 5,000 fish! Louise met Joan Carne, a streamkeeper volunteer, and the Stream of Dreams—

named by Chanel—was born. Community volunteers cut out thousands of fish from recycled plywood, schoolchildren painted them, and more volunteers tied the fish onto the fence around the abandoned lot.

It was a lot of work, but the result was stunning. Best of all, the children involved in the project heard the story of the storm-drain poisoning and learned about their *watershed*.

Other communities and schools asked for help making murals and teaching their students about watersheds, so Stream of Dreams Fish on Fences now swim around schoolyards and playgrounds elsewhere in Canada and in some US states.

19

Sockeye salmon spawning in the Grand Central River, AK.
CHRIS ZIMMERMAN/US GEOLOGICAL SURVEY

THE ONES THAT GET AWAY

The adult salmon that make it back to a river are the ones that get away—literally. They're the fish that escape all the dangers and survive to spawn. Biologists use the term *escapement* when they talk about the number of spawners heading upstream.

The chances of a salmon egg surviving to become a spawner are low. Only about one-half of fertilized eggs hatch. Around one-quarter of alevins become smolts. No more than one-tenth of smolts grow into silvery adulthood. And just one-twentieth of these adults make it back to their birthplace to spawn.

Time for some math? Let's say a redd starts with 5,000 fertilized eggs. If all goes well, 2,500 hatch as alevins, and 625 of these become smolts. About 60 of them grow into adults, and just 3 spawn the next generation. This is why salmon lay thousands of eggs—so that a few of them manage to complete the life cycle.

Survival rates from one stage to the next differ between salmon species. They even differ between populations of the same species.

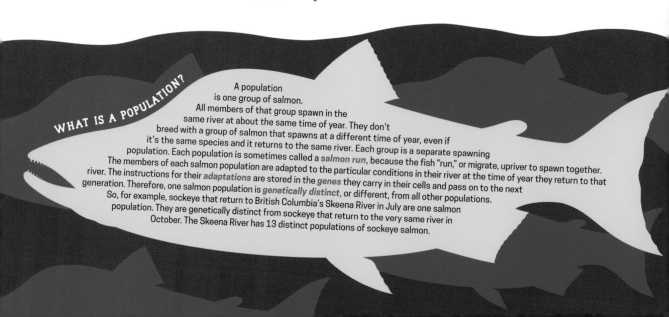

WHAT IS A POPULATION?

A population is one group of salmon. All members of that group spawn in the same river at about the same time of year. They don't breed with a group of salmon that spawns at a different time of year, even if it's the same species and it returns to the same river. Each group is a separate spawning population. Each population is sometimes called a *salmon run*, because the fish "run," or migrate, upriver to spawn together. The members of each salmon population are adapted to the particular conditions in their river at the time of year they return to that river. The instructions for their *adaptations* are stored in the *genes* they carry in their cells and pass on to the next generation. Therefore, one salmon population is *genetically distinct*, or different, from all other populations. So, for example, sockeye that return to British Columbia's Skeena River in July are one salmon population. They are genetically distinct from sockeye that return to the very same river in October. The Skeena River has 13 distinct populations of sockeye salmon.

Nozomi Aruga prepares to dissect a salmon for a group of students.
SAPPORO SALMON MUSEUM

JUMPING IN

Nozomi Aruga is curator and researcher at the Sapporo Salmon Museum in Japan, where she welcomes students from kindergarten to university. Depending on their age, students may examine salmon stuffies that open to show their insides, play board games about a salmon's life cycle or observe fish-dissection demonstrations. Students learn not just about the fish but about their stream habitats, including the *riparian* (streamside) ecosystem. Nozomi wants students to leave the museum knowing that Sapporo—a city of 2 million people—is richer for having salmon in its rivers. But to keep salmon returning, people have to give them the spaces they need.

> "I AM ENCOURAGING PEOPLE TO KNOW THE VALUE OF A WILD SALMON POPULATION IN A BIG CITY."
> —NOZOMI ARUGA

A hungry grizzly bear sneaks up on lunch in Katmai National Park, AK.
PAUL SOUDERS/GETTY IMAGES

3

AT THE HEART OF ECOSYSTEMS

I love living in a place with distinct seasons. I especially like walking in nature in the fall. The air feels crisp, the sun shines at an angle, colorful leaves float to the ground. I walk on—and the stench of rotting flesh wrinkles my nose. Whoa! What's that got to do with a fall walk in nature?

I forgot to mention that I'm walking near Goldstream River on Vancouver Island. Thousands of chum salmon spawn in this river in October and November. Some chinook and coho do too. The smell comes from a salmon carcass lying just off the path, its eyes pecked away and its belly half-eaten. As I watch, a seagull swoops down and resumes its meal.

SALMON LANDS

The death of thousands of salmon means smelly decomposing bodies. This brings huge quantities of nutrients like carbon, nitrogen and phosphorus into a watershed. Most of these nutrients are from the ocean, since that's where salmon do 90 percent or more of their growing. They bring

GO WILD

Salmonberry bushes grow from Alaska to Northern California and feed many bird and mammal species. The ripe berries are salmon-colored—pink, red or yellow—and the bushes themselves are often grown on nutrients from decaying salmon. Biologists have found that streams with more salmon carcasses have more salmonberry bushes growing alongside them.

so many marine nutrients to *terrestrial* (land) ecosystems that scientists consider salmon *ecosystem engineers*.

Algae, insects and other fish all benefit from these nutrients. So do the bald eagles and seabirds that gorge on the carcasses. Even little birds dip into the water and grab salmon eggs to eat. All these birds poop as they fly overhead, sending nutrients into the forest. Four-legged creatures—raccoons, otters, mink, shrews, bears—feed at the salmon buffet as well. More than 130 animal species eat salmon or their eggs. And, of course, these animals drag salmon carcasses into the forest and poop there too!

If a salmon population becomes extinct (dies out), then that population's birth stream no longer gets a yearly injection of ocean nutrients. The effects ripple through the ecosystem. For plants and animals, it's like not giving enough food to a child—they'll grow slower and be less healthy. Adults will reproduce less often or have fewer offspring. If a large river loses several salmon runs, the loss of nutrients can be immense, with devastating effects on both the aquatic and terrestrial ecosystems.

This coastal sea wolf has claimed a chum salmon carcass in the Great Bear Rainforest, BC.
© JOHN E MARRIOTT, WILDERNESSPRINTS.COM

Left: Salmon schooling in the Campbell River, BC. EIKO JONES

Right: Eiko Jones with some of his camera gear. Several of his underwater photos appear in the pages of this book. VIKTOR DAVARE

SALMON OCEANS

As well as contributing to terrestrial ecosystems, salmon play an important role in ocean *food webs*. They spend most of their lives in the ocean, and out there, they're lunch. For other species, that is. Many different marine mammals and fish eat salmon.

In the Atlantic Ocean, whales, seals, seabirds, sharks, tuna and other large fish eat salmon. How do scientists know what eats Atlantic salmon out in the ocean? They tag the salmon with small battery-powered devices that record data and send it to a satellite. The data includes the date, time, depth, light and temperature. If a tag records the lights going out during the daytime, then it's almost certainly because the fish got eaten. Using temperature data from tracking tags, scientists can get a good idea whether the predator is a cold-blooded fish like halibut or a warm-blooded fish like bluefin tuna or porbeagle shark.

JUMPING IN

When he was 14, Eiko Jones got his first camera and began photographing New Zealand's beautiful birdlife. Years later, living in western Canada, he landed a job as a river guide. But not for rafting or fishing—for snorkeling. Eiko took people snorkeling while salmon were migrating upstream. He became fascinated by salmon, got himself an underwater digital camera and began photographing salmon in rivers. Today he is an underwater photographer and filmmaker, and he also talks about watershed awareness at schools, where he sees young people's enthusiasm for the environment. "It gives me hope," he says, "that they'll carry that passion into the future."

> "MOST PEOPLE'S ONLY INTEREST IS TO EAT SALMON, BUT WE NEED TO SEE THEM AS MORE. THEY ARE INTEGRAL TO THE COAST."
> —EIKO JONES

Harbor seals live along coastlines of the northern hemisphere, in both the Atlantic and Pacific Oceans. They eat many types of fish, including salmon, and also other animals, such as squid, octopus, shrimp and clams.
ROLAND HEMMI/GETTY IMAGES

In the Pacific Ocean, too, salmon have lots of predators—whales, dolphins, seals, sea lions, other fish and, of course, people! Resident killer whales, or orcas, mainly eat salmon—chinook is their favorite. One adult orca needs 18 to 25 salmon per day. But with fewer chinook in the ocean, these mammals are finding it hard to eat enough fish to stay healthy. Salmon are an important part of the ocean food web, so when they're scarce, other parts of the food web can suffer.

AQUATIC CANARIES

In days gone by, coal miners took canaries underground. If dangerous gases started to build up below ground, the canary—which has more sensitive airways than humans—would stop singing or even collapse. The miners then knew they had to get out of the mine.

Salmon are canaries for their aquatic ecosystems, except biologists usually use the term *indicator species*. The behavior of an indicator species indicates, or tells us, something important about the health of the habitat it lives in.

Because salmon live in so many different habitats during their life cycle—freshwater estuary, nearshore, ocean—they are sensitive to changes in any of these locations. Salmon are sensitive to lots of things—water temperature (too warm?), water quality (cloudy or polluted?), predation (lots of big critters coming to eat them?). If salmon stop returning to streams to spawn, something's wrong. Something has damaged one or more of their habitats.

What kind of damage am I talking about? Let's step back in time and find out.

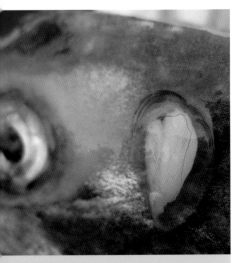

The white thing is an ear stone or otolith. Otoliths are found inside a fish's skull. This one has been extracted and placed on top of the fish for the photo. Otoliths grow as the fish grows, with new layers of material added over time. Just like they count rings in a tree trunk, biologists can count rings in an otolith to find out a fish's age.
SEAN BRENNAN

Mark Boyden in his workshop with the scale model he built of his local watershed. Note the "clouds" in the top left of the photo.
AMELIA BOYDEN

JUMPING IN

When Mark Boyden bought a piece of land in Ireland with salmon and trout streams on it, he started speaking out about water quality for fish. A lot of Ireland's streams—as in so many countries—have been damaged by urban growth, forestry and intensive agriculture. Mark helped start a program called StreamScapes and visited schools and community halls to talk with people about the watersheds they live in. He even built a 3D model of his local Coomhola River watershed, complete with "rainfall" from sprinkler heads hidden in "clouds." With this miniature but accurate model, people can see how water runs over land, into streams and to the sea.

"I'VE SEEN PEOPLE REALIZE HOW INTEGRAL THEY ARE WITH THE VALLEYS THEY LIVE IN, THE RIVERS THAT FLOW THROUGH THEIR COMMUNITIES, THE SALMON."

—MARK BOYDEN

Atlantic salmon leaping up a
waterfall in Newfoundland.
SHAUNL/GETTY IMAGES

4

ATLANTIC SALMON, THE LEAPING FISH

When I was a teenager, my dad took me to Scotland to visit his cousin Alfred. We took packages of smoked sockeye salmon with us as gifts. But we didn't know if Alfred's family ate fish, so before presenting them with the smoked salmon, my dad asked, "Do you like salmon?"

"Och, aye," Alfred replied.

My dad ventured further. "Have you ever had Pacific salmon?"

"Nay. Never 'ave, an' never will," Alfred said. "Atlantic salmon is the only fish for me."

My dad kept the sockeye in his suitcase, and he and I feasted on it later, while hiking in the Scottish Highlands.

For many people, like Alfred, the Atlantic salmon is the king of fish.

THE KING OF FISH

During the last ice age—which ended around 11,000 years ago—most of the current Atlantic salmon rivers didn't exist or were frozen to the bottom. Salmon avoided extinction by moving to a few southern refuge areas until

Hundreds of thousands of salmon used to swim in the Rhine River, which flows through populated and industrial regions of Europe, including Switzerland (photo) and Germany (inset wood engraving from 1893).
MAIN: © DIDIER MARTI/GETTY IMAGES
INSET: ZU_09/GETTY IMAGES

the ice melted. As rivers opened up again, salmon moved out of the refuges to populate more than 2,000 rivers in Europe and North America. Archaeologists (scientists who study past cultures) have found evidence from 40,000 to 48,000 years ago of early humans fishing for and eating salmon. A cave in France has a stone carving of a salmon, which archaeologists estimate is 25,000 years old.

We don't know how many Atlantic salmon swam in the ocean and returned to European rivers that long ago, but it would have been many millions of fish. More recently, in 1086, the Domesday Book recorded the results of a huge survey of resources in England and Wales. Many entries mention salmon fisheries, including some showing that salmon had value like money. For instance, one English lord received 1,000 salmon each year as a "tribute," meaning a payment.

As well as catching salmon, people changed salmon habitats by placing dams, weirs and watermills on rivers. These structures benefited people but stopped salmon from reaching their spawning grounds, harming salmon populations. Even in the 11th century, some European countries already had laws to protect salmon. King Malcolm II of Scotland was one of the first rulers to set up specific times during the year when people could and couldn't fish.

The Rhine River—the longest river in western Europe—flows through Switzerland, Germany and the Netherlands. It once had the largest number of Atlantic salmon in Europe, but by the 1950s, salmon had disappeared from this river. This story repeats for many of Europe's salmon rivers. What happened to the fish?

Molly Woodring explores nature with young kids.
MAINE AUDUBON

THE HUMAN MACHINE

In the mid-1700s, the *Industrial Revolution* in Europe changed conditions for salmon and their rivers. The Industrial Revolution began with the invention of the steam engine, which powered paper, flour and cotton mills as well as other industries. By the end of the 1800s, big factories were releasing chemicals and other industrial wastes into streams and rivers. Sewage from growing cities also went into rivers. More and more dams were built to generate *hydropower* and divert water for urban and agricultural uses.

As steam-powered boats began to ply rivers, the river channels were straightened into canals to make them safer

JUMPING IN

Molly Woodring works for Maine Audubon, where she participates in Fish Friends, an educational program run by the Atlantic Salmon Federation. She introduces kids as young as three and four to ecosystems. They read stories, create art, explore pond life outdoors and check out salmon eggs incubating in a tank. For Molly, it's all about helping kids—and their parents—see connections in nature and think about the bigger picture.

"SALMON ARE THESE GREAT CONNECTORS BY GOING BETWEEN FRESH WATER AND MARINE ECOSYSTEMS."
—MOLLY WOODRING

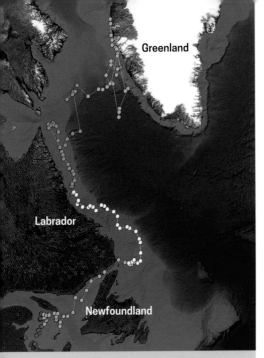

Scientists can follow salmon by implanting or attaching tracking devices that send location information to a satellite. This map shows the northward swim of one Atlantic salmon kelt (a fish that has already spawned) after it left the Miramichi River in New Brunswick. Each dot color is for a different consecutive month, starting with pink for May.
ATLANTIC SALMON FEDERATION

to navigate. These efforts stripped the rivers of their streamside vegetation, removed side channels and often destroyed spawning areas for salmon.

Fisheries also netted huge numbers of salmon, either in the river or where the fish gathered in river estuaries before swimming upstream to spawn. Fishing boats and gear got more efficient at scooping up fish, and overfishing became rampant. On the Tweed River in Scotland, fishers in the 1730s were taking 1,000 to 2,000 salmon each year. By the 1790s, they were hauling out 10,000 to 20,000 per year. With fewer mature fish left to spawn the next generation, the population shrank. By 1850 people were able to catch only a few hundred salmon from the Tweed River.

With so many pressures, the number of salmon returning to spawn in most European rivers became smaller and smaller.

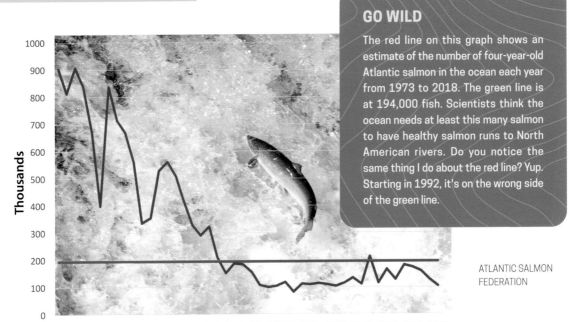

GO WILD

The red line on this graph shows an estimate of the number of four-year-old Atlantic salmon in the ocean each year from 1973 to 2018. The green line is at 194,000 fish. Scientists think the ocean needs at least this many salmon to have healthy salmon runs to North American rivers. Do you notice the same thing I do about the red line? Yup. Starting in 1992, it's on the wrong side of the green line.

ATLANTIC SALMON FEDERATION

Adult Atlantic salmon in a Quebec river.
NICK HAWKINS

ACROSS THE OCEAN

Meanwhile, in North America, Indigenous Peoples along the East Coast from present-day New York State to northern Labrador lived alongside Atlantic salmon and many other fish species, including eels, shad and bass. The plentiful fish were a major part of the diet in many communities. People caught salmon with spears, nets and bone hooks, and they smoked and dried the fish to preserve it for later in the year when the salmon runs were over. The Indigenous Peoples living on the East Coast also held ceremonies to thank the salmon for returning to the rivers each year. For example, Mi'kmaq always place fish bones and other remains back in the river out of respect for the animal's spirit. Their cultures were based on using natural resources in a way that revered and honored them.

Mi'kmaq people with fishing rods and canoes.
G.T. TAYLOR/NOVA SCOTIA ARCHIVES

When English, French and Portuguese explorers arrived on the eastern shores of North America in the late 1400s and early 1500s, they were astonished by the abundance of

Eelgrass meadows are an important habitat for young salmon, but invasive crabs are disrupting them. For more about invasive crabs in coastal waters, see page 77. NICK HAWKINS

JUMPING IN

On Prince Edward Island, where Randy Angus works with the Mi'kmaq Confederacy of PEI, one of the biggest challenges is keeping rivers and coastal marshes salmon friendly. The island province is an agricultural center—farmland covers nearly 600,000 acres (243,000 hectares), or three times the area of New York City! During storms, rainwater runs over the fields and carries soil, fertilizers and pesticides straight into the rivers and marshes. And when it gets windy, soil blows off the fields and into the water. There the soil particles settle, choking fish eggs and covering algae. Fertilizers contain nutrients that boost the growth of undesirable algae, and pesticides poison both plants and creatures.

Randy and his team recently began a project to protect and restore eelgrass meadows in coastal marshes. The eelgrasses take up nutrients from agricultural runoff. And they help with other problems too. Eelgrasses form natural barriers along the shore to lessen the force of pounding waves on coastal habitats, and they provide refuge and feeding habitat for juvenile fish—including Atlantic salmon.

"THE ENVIRONMENTAL INSULTS ARE UNBELIEVABLE."
—RANDY ANGUS

animals and fish, including salmon. European settlers soon began arriving by the boatload. They fished the salmon to eat, to sell and even to plow into their fields as fertilizer. By the late 1700s, the populations of Atlantic salmon were clearly declining. Just like in Europe, settlers in the British colonies (today's Canadian Atlantic provinces) and in the newly formed United States of America had overfished, built dams and cleared the land alongside rivers.

By the late 1800s, the only eastern state with salmon was Maine, with about 500,000 returning to spawn each year. In 1947 only 400 salmon were caught in Maine, and in 1948 commercial fishing of Atlantic salmon stopped in the United States.

Strong salmon runs remained for longer in eastern Canada, but their numbers soon declined too. In 1984 Canada shut down most of its commercial Atlantic salmon fisheries, and by 2000 they had all been stopped. However, enough fish still return for Indigenous food fisheries and sportfishing to continue on many rivers.

A river winding through fields on Prince Edward Island. BLAINE HARRINGTON III/GETTY IMAGES

Randy Angus looks at eelgrasses growing below the water surface. LORI HASLETT

Atlantic salmon swimming
beneath river ice.
NICK HAWKINS

WILD ATLANTIC SALMON TODAY

Wild Atlantic salmon as a species is a shadow of its former self. Somewhat healthy wild populations still exist in some European streams, including ones in Russia, Norway, Finland, Scotland and Ireland. However, most wild salmon populations in Europe are struggling at best, and many have become extinct. In North America, at least one Atlantic salmon population has recently become extinct and most of the rest are endangered and struggling to survive.

Many people who work with salmon worry that the collapse of wild Atlantic salmon populations will soon be repeated with salmon in the Pacific.

GO WILD

In 2019 about 435,000 Atlantic salmon returned to Canadian rivers, one of the lowest numbers in the past 50 years. In the same year, US rivers—all of them in Maine—had only about 1,500 adult salmon.

These coho salmon are migrating up a river to spawn. At this stage in their life cycle, male coho get an especially hooked nose, like the one closest to the camera. The fish behind him are female. EIKO JONES

5
PACIFIC SALMON, THE HOOK-NOSED FISH

I once interviewed for a job in a government fisheries department. I was asked to name the five salmon species in the Pacific Northwest of North America. At first I could remember only four, but eventually the fifth popped into my mind. Phew!

When I was writing this book, one of the people I spoke with gave me a mnemonic (a memory aid). All you need is your hand.

- Your thumb rhymes with chum.
- Your index finger can poke out an eye, so is for sockeye.
- Your middle finger is the biggest, so is for king (chinook).
- Your ring finger wears shiny jewelry, so is for silver (coho).
- Your little finger is a pinky, so is for pink.

It would have been handy (haha) to know this mnemonic during that job interview years ago.

Indigenous Ainu people in about 1950.
THREE LIONS/GETTY IMAGES

The Pacific Ocean is home to six species of wild salmon. One of them—masu or cherry salmon—lives only on the Russian and Far East Asian side. There are no masu salmon on the North American side.
KENTARO MORITA

THE PLACE WITH SIX SALMON

The Pacific salmon species are all pretty young—that is, they evolved into the species we know today between 10 and 6 million years ago (in evolution, that's recent). Ten million years ago, the masu salmon became a distinct species (as did the steelhead rainbow trout, which is closely related to Pacific salmon). Then, by about 6 million years ago, the other five species became distinct—chinook, coho, pink, chum and sockeye.

The masu salmon live only on the western side of the Pacific Ocean. They're mainly around the Sea of Japan and in the Sea of Okhotsk, spawning in rivers in northern Japan, North and South Korea and parts of Russia. In Japan the masu are called sakura masu, or cherry salmon—so named because some populations migrate back to their river in spring when the cherry blossoms are out. They then fast until the fall, when they spawn.

About 16,500 years ago, the Jōmon people in Japan foraged for plants, hunted land animals and also fished. To catch salmon, they used traps and spears. The Ainu people, who are descended from the Jōmon, still live on Japan's northern island of Hokkaido, where they honor the first returning salmon of the year with a ceremony. The Ainu call salmon *shipe*, which means "staple food" in their language.

BECOMING SALMON PEOPLE

In the most recent ice age, Earth had so much water frozen in glaciers that sea level dropped. A flat, grassy plain stretched between today's Russia and today's Alaska. According to Western science, Indigenous Peoples migrated from west to east across this land bridge—known as Beringia—and populated Alaska and the

About one-quarter of all Pacific salmon spawn in rivers on Russia's Kamchatka Peninsula.
EASTIMAGES/GETTY IMAGES

Pacific Northwest of North America. When the glaciers began melting, the sea level rose and cut off the land bridge about 11,600 years ago.

These first people in Alaska were likely foragers and hunters who ate fish and shellfish when they got a chance to catch or collect them. The first known salmon fishing was on the Yukon River. There archaeologists found chum salmon bones at people's campsites from about 11,500 years ago.

Farther south, on the Columbia and Fraser Rivers, Indigenous Peoples were fishing for salmon by about 8,000 years ago. These rivers are the largest in the Pacific Northwest, and they both have narrow sections where people can stand on rocks to fish with nets or spears. Historians think that salmon was just one of many foods eaten by people at that time. But over thousands of years, salmon became more important to Indigenous Peoples. Around 3,000 years ago, the people in the Pacific

GO WILD
When glaciers were at their largest during the last ice age, about 18,000 years ago, most of what we know as Alaska and British Columbia was under ice. But a few *refugia* (refuges for plants and animals) stayed ice-free. Pacific salmon survived in these refugia, and when the ice melted, they expanded their range to populate newly formed rivers.

A Quinault woman preparing salmon.
JOEL W. ROGERS/GETTY IMAGES

Northwest began smoking and drying salmon to eat later in the year. Salmon trading also began. The Chinookan Peoples traded chinook salmon (also called king salmon) from the Columbia River with Indigenous people as far away as the Great Plains.

Salmon became deeply engrained in Indigenous cultures throughout the Pacific Northwest. Their relationships with salmon run deep and include catching, eating and trading salmon, as well as honoring and caring for them. Indigenous Peoples then and now see the world as interconnected, including both animate and inanimate parts of nature. Everything in the world is related and must be cared for. A woman from the Haida Nation explained it to me like this: Look out for and respect your relatives, and they will do the same for you.

The Pacific Northwest wasn't an untouched wilderness in the days before European explorers and settlers arrived. It was a land with Indigenous Peoples who followed laws about how, when and where to use natural resources—like harvesting salmon. The land was governed by people who took but also gave back.

Indigenous fishers working a salmon weir on the Cowichan River, Vancouver Island, BC.
ANTHONY CARTER/COURTESY OF UBC MUSEUM OF ANTHROPOLOGY/IMG#A038180

For some of her work, Andrea Reid captures salmon using a Nisga'a fish wheel—an ancient technology that traps fish gently.
NICOLE MORVEN

ALEX SARNA

"IF ELDERS WHO HAVE
SEEN SO MANY CHANGES
IN THEIR LIFETIMES
CAN HAVE HOPE, THEN
I HAVE HOPE TOO."

—ANDREA REID

JUMPING IN

Andrea Reid belongs to the Nisga'a Nation on the West Coast of Canada. She grew up on the East Coast in Mi'kma'ki, which are the homelands of the Mi'kmaq. From Mi'kmaq Elders, she learned about Two-Eyed Seeing— you'll remember that means observing a situation with one eye open to Indigenous knowledge and the other open to Western knowledge.

Andrea is now a fisheries scientist at the University of British Columbia, and she's using Two-Eyed Seeing in her studies. She gathers scientific information about sockeye salmon by measuring fish, checking their health and tagging them with a radio transmitter to track their swim upstream. She also learns by asking Indigenous knowledge holders and Elders about their experiences fishing for sockeye—both now and in the past. By gathering and studying all this information, Andrea is "seeing with both eyes" as she pieces together a fuller picture of migrating sockeye and how people could improve their survival.

Andrea uses a radio device to track the salmon she tags as they leave the ocean.
COLLIN MIDDLETON

A load of salmon on the Fraser River, BC, in about 1900.
STEPHEN JOSEPH THOMPSON/CITY OF VANCOUVER ARCHIVES/AM1376-: CVA 137-80

EXPLORERS AND SETTLERS TRAVEL WEST

The first Europeans and eastern Americans to see the Pacific Northwest were wowed by the powerful rivers and great numbers of salmon. But they didn't exploit the salmon initially. They had their eyes set on beaver and sea-otter furs and, especially, on gold.

The region's first gold rush happened along the Sacramento and other rivers in California. Later, gold miners went north to the Fraser River in British Columbia and the Klondike River in Yukon. Gold mining damaged rivers by clearing away streamside vegetation, filling them with silt and other debris and polluting the water. Since salmon need clean gravel to spawn in and cool water for their juveniles to live in, the damage from gold mining harmed many salmon populations.

Other activities affected the salmon's freshwater habitat too. Settlers cut trees to build roads and homes, cleared land to farm and tapped into rivers to extract water. Starting in the 1880s, they began building large dams to generate hydropower. Commercial salmon fishing began in the 1800s, too, using traps set in bays or the *mouths* of rivers and, later, nets towed by powerboats. Much of the catch was packed in salt barrels and exported to Hawaii, eastern North America and Europe. Soon a new way to preserve and ship salmon came to the Pacific Northwest— the cannery.

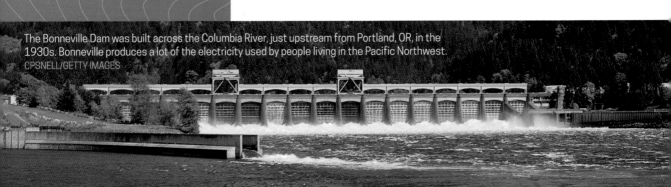

The Bonneville Dam was built across the Columbia River, just upstream from Portland, OR, in the 1930s. Bonneville produces a lot of the electricity used by people living in the Pacific Northwest.
CPSNELL/GETTY IMAGES

Canneries were typically built on stilts over the water for quick access to the loads of salmon being brought in.
IMAGE C-08605 COURTESY OF THE ROYAL BC MUSEUM

Women packing salmon into cans at a cannery in Prince Rupert, BC, in 1941.
STEFFENS-COLMER STUDIOS LTD AND DON COLTMAN COMPANY PHOTOGRAPHS/ CITY OF VANCOUVER ARCHIVES/ AM1545-S3-: CVA 586-699

A label for a can of salmon.
IMAGE I-61133 COURTESY OF THE ROYAL BC MUSEUM

CANNERIES

Canning got its start in Europe when Napoleon Bonaparte, a French military leader, offered a prize for inventing a good way to preserve food. Napoleon needed to feed his armies with a portable food that would not rot. A French chef won the prize, but the English turned canning into an industry.

Canning came first to eastern North America and then to the west in 1864, when a salmon cannery opened on California's Sacramento River. Within a few years, this river didn't have enough salmon left, so the cannery moved to the Columbia River. The number of canneries grew, and they pumped out thousands of cans of salmon every year. In 1880 Oregon alone had 55 canneries that produced 500,000 cans of salmon! More canneries opened in Washington, British Columbia and Alaska. Salmon canning became a major industry.

In the first salmon canneries, people chopped up salmon and put the meat into cans by hand. Many of the workers were Indigenous women and Chinese immigrants.

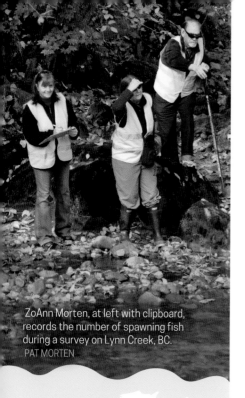

ZoAnn Morten, at left with clipboard, records the number of spawning fish during a survey on Lynn Creek, BC.
PAT MORTEN

Later, machines took over some of the work. Cannery owners bought vast quantities of salmon from fishers to make sure they wouldn't run out. But a lot of the time, some of the salmon rotted before they could be processed.

WILD PACIFIC SALMON TODAY

Pacific salmon no longer pile up and rot on the wharves outside cannery buildings. But we still treat salmon (and other organisms) as less important than people. As a result, many Pacific salmon populations are in real trouble.

On both sides of the Pacific Ocean, salmon are doing especially poorly toward the southern end of their range.

- In Canada and the United States, dozens of salmon populations are listed as endangered or threatened.

- In Washington, Idaho, Oregon and California, about 40 percent of salmon and oceangoing trout populations are extinct. For every 10 streams, only 6 of them still have salmon (or anadromous trout).

- In British Columbia, sockeye salmon populations returning to the Fraser River—the province's largest river system—have all but collapsed.

- Most chinook populations in these locations are declining, as are quite a few coho populations.

- In China and Russia, some chum populations are badly depleted or no longer exist in rivers where they once did. The Amur River, which forms much of the border between China and Russia, has been heavily fished for more than a century and now has many threatened fish populations.

- On the Kamchatka Peninsula in Russia, sockeye, coho and masu populations are threatened.

- In Japan, most pink salmon populations are no longer wild. They're mainly *hatchery* fish that are stocked into rivers annually in time to go out to sea.

Other Pacific salmon populations are doing better. Many, though not all, chum and pink populations seem to be healthy. And in the north, especially in Alaska, large salmon runs still return to rivers each year. Bristol Bay, which is nestled above the Aleutian Island chain, has many salmon rivers draining into it. About 40 million salmon return to these rivers each year, a lot of them sockeye.

Throughout the Pacific Ocean, pink salmon are doing the best and chinook the worst. The overall picture is certainly better for Pacific salmon than for Atlantic salmon. But this may not last for long unless we address some of the many problems we've thrown in the path of wild salmon.

Read on to find out about the threats salmon have faced both in the Atlantic and in the Pacific, and some of the things people are doing to help.

A school of pink salmon. EIKO JONES

Common name	Atlantic salmon	Masu salmon, cherry salmon	Chum salmon, dog salmon	Pink salmon, humpbacks, humpies
Latin name	*Salmo salar*	*Oncorhynchus masou*	*Oncorhynchus keta*	*Oncorhynchus gorbuscha*
Region	Northwest and northeast Atlantic	Northwest Pacific	Northwest and northeast Pacific	Northwest and northeast Pacific
Time juveniles spend in fresh water	About 2 years (but up to 5 years in far northern rivers)	1 to 3 years in rivers	Days to a few months in rivers	Days to a few months in rivers
Typical weight at maturity	After 2 years at sea: 10–20 pounds (4.5–9 kg) but some can be as heavy as 30 pounds (13.6 kg)	4.5–5.5 pounds (2–2.5 kg)	6.5–13 pounds (3–6 kg)	3.5–5.5 pounds (1.5–2.5 kg)
Typical length at maturity	After 2 years at sea: About 30 inches (76 cm)	20 inches (51 cm)	24–32 inches (61–81 cm)	18–22 inches (46–56 cm)
Lifespan (age at spawning)	3 or 4 years (at first spawning) with lifespan of 3 to 7 years, with a maximum of about 11 years	2 to 4 years	3 or 4 years	2 years
Appearance as a spawner	Bronze color	Pink and red vertical stripes	Green and purple vertical bars	Pale gray. Males get a huge humped back

WESTEND61/GETTY IMAGES

KENTARO MORITA

EIKO JONES

EIKO JONES

Fish Facts	Six-inch-long (15-cm) smolts can swim up to 17 miles (27 km) each day	Spend only one year in the sea	Make the longest migrations of all Pacific salmon	The most abundant salmon in the Pacific Ocean
	Adults can jump nearly 12 feet (3.7 m) to get over an obstacle	Have short ocean migrations	The poorest jumpers of all Pacific salmon	Have the lowest oil content of the Pacific salmon

Common name	Sockeye salmon, red salmon	Chinook salmon, king salmon, spring salmon, tyee	Coho salmon, silver salmon, blueback
Latin name	*Oncorhynchus nerka*	*Oncorhynchus tshawytscha*	*Oncorhynchus kisutch*
Region	Northwest and northeast Pacific	Northwest and northeast Pacific	Northwest and northeast Pacific
Time juveniles spend in fresh water	1 to 3 years, usually in a lake	Months up to 2 years in rivers	1 to 2 years in rivers
Typical weight at maturity	3.5–8 pounds (1.6–3.6 kg)	11–50+ pounds (5–23+ kg)	5.5—11 pounds (2.5–5 kg)
Typical length at maturity	18–26 inches (46–66 cm)	27–60 inches (69–152 cm)	24–38 inches (61–95 cm)
Lifespan (age at spawning)	4 to 5 years	3 to 7 years	2 to 4 years
Appearance as a spawner	Bright red with an olive-green head. Males get a humped back	Deep red to coppery black	Red belly with a dark back. Male's nose deeply hooked, and mouth won't close
	EIKO JONES	EIKO JONES	EIKO JONES
Fish Facts	Spawn in lakes, on beaches or in rivers	Largest of the Pacific salmon— some weigh in at more than 100 pounds (45 kg)	Eat a lot of shrimp in the ocean
	Have especially large runs of spawning fish every four years	Strong swimmers and impressive leapers	Juveniles like pools and side channels in rivers

A fishing boat sets a seine net to catch salmon migrating along coastal Vancouver Island. One-half to three-quarters of the salmon caught commercially are pink salmon. Chum and sockeye make up most of the rest.
JOEL W. ROGERS/GETTY IMAGES

6

FISH OUT
OF WATER

When I was a kid growing up in Vancouver, British Columbia, one of my favorite Saturday-morning excursions was to Granville Island and its public market. It sells every kind of food, from cheese to chocolate, fruit to fish. The island has docks where fishers can sell their catch right from their boat. You can't get fish much fresher than that!

Fishing—also called harvesting—is an age-old practice that has turned into a worldwide industry. It's one of a long list of human activities that can threaten the existence of wild fish populations, including salmon. Biologists often say salmon are threatened by four Hs of human activity: harvest, habitat (both freshwater and ocean), hydropower and hatcheries. Another threat, related to but distinct from hatcheries, is salmon farming. And overlying all of these is climate change.

Phew! What a lot of threats for a fish to face. Let's start with harvest.

Fishers hauling up their nets. Can you see the salmon they've caught?
THOMAS BARWICK/GETTY IMAGES

SET THE NETS

Harvesting or fishing isn't a bad thing when it's done responsibly. Fishing provides employment, often in small communities along coastlines. Fishing provides food—a particularly healthy food too.

Biologists name harvest as one of their four Hs because of *over*harvesting or *over*fishing. Overfishing is a problem in oceans and rivers around the globe. Many people and countries are greedy. We often take too many fish and we do it too fast. We don't give nature time to replace the fish to keep fish populations healthy.

Many, many fish species are in this boat (sad pun, but true!). Scientists estimate that more than 30 percent of the world's fish populations are overfished. Sixty percent of fish populations are "fully fished"—meaning that the current harvest is all the population can handle. If the population stays the same size and the catch increases, then they could join the ranks of the overfished.

HARVEST IN THE ATLANTIC OCEAN

Overfishing can eventually cause a population to collapse. Then there are no more fish to fish. One example is the Atlantic cod. They have been fished by countries on both sides of the Atlantic Ocean for hundreds of years, but by the early 1990s, Atlantic cod off the East Coast of North America had nearly disappeared. There were so few fish that Canada closed its commercial (for sale) cod fishery in 1993, and it hasn't reopened. Elsewhere, such as in Iceland and Norway, cod populations are in better health, and fisheries continue.

Another example is the Atlantic salmon. The number of fish declined to such a low number that most commercial fishing stopped in the mid- or late-1900s in both Europe and North America. However, fishers from Greenland continued a commercial harvest of Atlantic salmon until recently. This fishery was controversial, since the fish being caught had hatched in European and North American rivers, not Greenland rivers. Greenland itself has only one river with a wild salmon population. In 2018 Greenland agreed to a 12-year moratorium—which is a break in activity—on commercial fishing of Atlantic salmon.

This sockeye salmon is from Bristol Bay in Alaska, which has the world's largest sockeye salmon fishery. Not only that, more sockeye are caught in Bristol Bay alone than in the rest of the world's sockeye fisheries combined. (We tried to find a photo showing commercial fishing for wild Atlantic salmon, but we came up short. Most of these fisheries stopped many decades ago.)
ED BENNETT / DESIGN PICS/GETTY IMAGES

Commercial fishing boats typically fish for salmon in one of three ways. In the early days of commercial fishing, fishers set and pulled in their nets and lines by hand. Today most fishing boats have sophisticated winches and other machinery to help set and bring in the gear.
BC SALMON MARKETING COUNCIL AND MARINE STEWARDSHIP COUNCIL

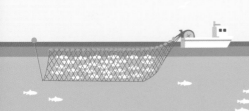

Gillnetting
A net hangs in the water. When fish swim into it, their gills get caught in the mesh.

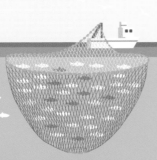

Seining
A net is set in a circle and then the bottom edges are pulled together to trap fish inside.

Trolling
Long lines with hooks are pulled—or trolled—through the water.

Standing in their gillnet boat, Kris Nakashima, at left, and his father and brother each hold a freshly caught chum salmon.
BC SALMON MARKETING COUNCIL

JUMPING IN

Kris Nakashima was 14 when he began helping as a deckhand on his dad's salmon-fishing boat in the lower Fraser River. "It was a great summer job," he says, "except I got sick a lot at the beginning." Feeling seasick didn't deter Kris, though. He was inspired to keep going out on the boat because fishing is part of his family history. His grandfather fished salmon and lingcod for a living, and his father and uncle both fished and opened a fishing-gear store. Today Kris and his brother do the same—fish for salmon and run the store. Kris loves fishing, not only because it provides for his family and offers him challenging work, but also because of the tight community of fishers. "The people are second to none," he says.

> "WE HAVE THIS BEAUTIFUL RESOURCE, A FOOD SOURCE THAT'S COMPLETELY NATURAL. IT'S A MATTER OF RESPECTING IT TO HARVEST IT."
> —KRIS NAKASHIMA

HARVEST IN THE PACIFIC OCEAN

In the Pacific Ocean, commercial salmon fishing began, as elsewhere in the world, with fishers setting their nets by hand from wooden boats. Over time it has become fleets of large boats with machinery to operate the nets and massive refrigerators and freezers to store the fish. As the industry grew and changed, it became more and more difficult for each of the five countries with Pacific salmon rivers—United States, Canada, Russia, Japan and Korea—to agree on how many fish they each got to harvest. Arguments erupted about who was fishing whose salmon.

To stop the disputes and instead work together to promote salmon conservation and sustainable fisheries, these five countries set up the North Pacific Anadromous Fish Commission (NPAFC), which took effect in 1993. Each country reports its salmon harvest to this organization, which tracks the numbers. The NPAFC also collected the harvest numbers from each country going back as far as 1925. These numbers show that over the past century, more than 100 million Pacific salmon have been caught each year. In some recent years, salmon catches have been as high as 600 million fish in a single year!

ALL MIXED UP

Traditionally, many Indigenous fisheries were in rivers, often near salmon spawning grounds. This way people fished only one population of salmon at a time. They used dip nets, fish wheels and other methods that caught some fish and let others swim past. Coastal peoples used reef nets near the mouth of rivers to selectively catch migrating salmon.

After settlers arrived in North America, they set up governments to decide who could fish, when and where they could fish, what methods they could use to fish and how many fish they could take. Colonial governments prohibited Indigenous Peoples from using their traditional fishing methods and instead allowed commercial fishers to catch salmon at sea. Salmon fishing became a big industry, with fleets of boats catching huge quantities of fish to sell all over the world.

Commercial boats often catch fish where many different salmon populations can be swimming together in the ocean. Boats set nets to catch fish from a strong salmon population—one that has lots of adult fish. But if a salmon population with fewer fish is swimming along

IAN DYBALL/GETTY IMAGES

Wild-capture fisheries can choose to be evaluated against the Marine Stewardship Council (MSC) Fisheries Standard. Seafood with the blue MSC label is from a well-managed and sustainable fishery. More than 400 fisheries in the world are certified with this standard.
LOGOS: MARINE STEWARDSHIP COUNCIL
PACKAGING: VLAD KLOK/SHUTTERSTOCK.COM

Reefnet fishing for salmon is a longtime Indigenous fishing method in the Salish Sea.
EDMUND LOWE PHOTOGRAPHY/GETTY IMAGES

at the same time, these fish get scooped up too. Fishing where several salmon populations are swimming together is called a mixed-stock fishery (*stock* is another word for *population*). Mixed-stock fisheries can be a big problem for many struggling salmon populations.

Today there's growing awareness that if we want healthy salmon populations in the future, we need to change how we fish. Fishing practices need to be sustainable, similar to the way Indigenous communities fished traditionally. Indigenous fisheries took place for thousands of years before settlers arrived, and during that time salmon populations stayed healthy. Clearly those communities were doing something right!

We can all do something right by being thoughtful consumers. In a store or restaurant, I now always ask where and how a salmon—or any fish—is caught and only buy ones that come from sustainable fisheries. Sustainable fisheries aim to keep fish populations healthy and seafood available for future generations. Smaller, local and more selective salmon fisheries are already gaining ground (or water!), both in rivers and in coastal areas. These fisheries need our support.

INDIGENOUS FISHING METHODS

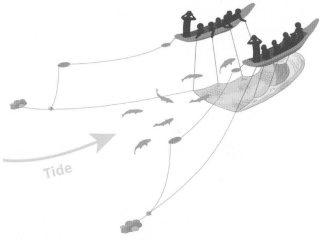

Weirs are fences built across rivers or streams. A weir has a small opening or a trap where fishers can catch salmon as the fish pass through on their way upstream.

Stone fish traps are built near the mouth of a river, because salmon often wait in the estuary before swimming upstream. As the tide comes in, the salmon move closer to shore. Then, as the tide goes out, some of them get trapped.

Reef nets are set in shallow ocean water. Two nets extend from the ends of two boats and are anchored to the seafloor. They funnel migrating salmon into a central net that fishers can lift to catch the fish.

Dip nets are nets on long poles that fishers typically use in narrow river canyons and near waterfalls. In these places, migrating salmon often swim close to the river edge and can be scooped from the water.

Fish wheels are floating platforms with mesh baskets. The flow of the river turns the wheel, and the baskets scoop salmon from the water and funnel them into a holding box.

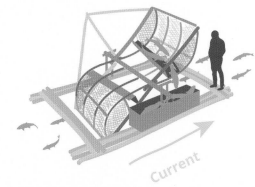

THE TEXT HAS BEEN ADAPTED FROM THE ORIGINAL FOR THIS BOOK'S AUDIENCE.
BIOSCIENCE, VOLUME 71, ISSUE 2, FEBRUARY 2021, PAGES 186–204,
HTTPS://DOI.ORG/10.1093/BIOSCI/BIAA144

Lower Elwha member Peyton Cable participates in the annual First Salmon ceremony, a ritual of harvest.
E. TAMMY KIM

An Indigenous man fishing for salmon with a dip net in the 1940s.
IMAGE D-06014 COURTESY OF
THE ROYAL BC MUSEUM

INDIGENOUS FISHING RIGHTS

Over thousands of years of fishing for salmon, Indigenous Peoples have developed strong connections to these fish. People work hard and fast for the few weeks of a salmon run to catch and preserve enough fish to feed the community all winter. They hold ceremonies to thank and honor the salmon. Years ago, they traded salmon with other Indigenous Peoples and with settlers. Now Indigenous-run companies sell fish and Indigenous nations fish to be able to distribute food to their community members.

Indigenous Peoples in North America have inherent rights to fish for salmon, meaning that they have the right to fish because their ancestors fished on these lands long before Europeans arrived. Indigenous Peoples never gave up their rights to fish, but colonial governments have often ignored them. In 1974 the Supreme Court of the United States delivered a ruling, called the Boldt Decision, that recognized Indigenous fishing rights. In 1990 Canada's Supreme Court heard the Sparrow case and made a similar ruling. Even so, confrontations still occur between different groups of people who all want to catch salmon.

Kari Alex, in sunglasses, and her coworkers fish with a seine net in the Okanagan River, BC. OKANAGAN NATION ALLIANCE

JUMPING IN

Historically the Okanagan Valley had a strong sockeye salmon population. The fish swam from the Pacific Ocean up the Columbia River and then up the Okanogan (US spelling) River into British Columbia. From there the fish swam north through a chain of lakes connected by the Okanagan River. But then European settlers arrived and altered the Columbia and Okanagan watersheds by removing vast quantities of water, straightening sections of the river and building dams. The sockeye could make it to a lake on the Canada–US border, but no farther.

So in the late 1990s, Okanagan Nation Alliance began kł cṗəlk̓ stim̓ (cause to come back), a project that uses western science and Traditional Knowledge to restore salmon. Syilx knowledge keepers and Elders directed Kari Alex and other fish biologists as they restored river habitat and built passageways over dams. The biologists also helped to develop the Fish Water Management Tool—a computer software program for figuring out how much water can be taken for people and agriculture without drying up fish eggs in the gravel.

In 2004 the Okanagan Nation started seeding a lake partway up the chain with sockeye fry. With a passable path up the river, adult salmon can now make it farther into British Columbia than they have in more than 50 years. In 2020 sockeye finally had access to the last lake in the chain and the largest in the valley. And Okanagan Nation members once again have an active food fishery for sockeye salmon.

"THE SALMON RETURNING HAS GIVEN A LOT OF HOPE. WE WEREN'T SURE IT WAS POSSIBLE. WE'RE CONSTANTLY SURPRISED."

—KARI ALEX

A fisher removes the eggs from a chinook salmon caught in the Feather River, CA. The fish in this photo was not poached, though.
BARBARA RICH/GETTY IMAGES

My younger daughter, Madeleine, holds a coho salmon caught in the ocean off the west coast of Vancouver Island, BC.
ANDREW WILSON

FISHING FOR FUN

Many people enjoy sport or recreational fishing for salmon. Some sportfishers go out on the ocean with rods and lines to catch salmon in nearshore waters. Other sportfishers prefer to fish with a flexible rod that casts a long line far out into a river. At the end of the line is a hook dressed up with fibers and feathers to attract salmon. Even though salmon stop eating when they enter rivers, they will still grab at a lure. This sport is called fly-fishing, and it's popular for catching both Atlantic and Pacific salmon.

In the North Pacific countries, sportfishers catch only one salmon for every 150 caught by commercial fishers. But sportfishing brings money into small communities—often quite a lot of money. When people go out for a day of fishing, they don't just fish. They buy things like a fishing license, fishing gear, clothing, gas for their vehicle, a meal, maybe even a night in a hotel. The ripple effect of sportfishing means that a single salmon caught with a rod on a river can be worth more than $1,000 for the economy.

For many people who fly-fish, the experience is as much about being in nature as it is about landing a big fish, though that's exhilarating too. Being in the natural habitat of animals and plants brings people peace and joy, and it comes with responsibilities. Too often people treat nature poorly, which is why habitat—specifically habitat damage—is the second of the four Hs that threaten salmon.

Todd Karnas, in the blue shirt, casts on the Codroy River, NL. He says he'll never forget the first time an Atlantic salmon grabbed the fly on the end of his line: "You would swear that the salmon meets your eye directly and challenges you to a tussle." JENNY HATT

Todd uses nine different materials, including white moose hair and a feather from a golden pheasant to tie this fly, called a White-Wing Blue Charm.
TODD KARNAS

JUMPING IN

Todd Karnas likes nothing better than to get up before sunrise, grab his waders and fly rod, and head out to a Newfoundland river to fly-fish for Atlantic salmon. Out on the river, he finds himself immersed in the environment and having to use his wits, not power, to catch a fish. Todd's love of fly-fishing led him to help out in a fly shop, where he learned to tie his own flies—the feather, hair, thread, silk and tinsel creations that attract a salmon. He now guides trips for people who want to try their hand at fly-fishing.

"GET OUTDOORS AND HAVE FUN. INTERACT WITH THESE ECOSYSTEMS AND DETERMINE YOUR RELATIONSHIP AND OBLIGATIONS TO THEM."
—TODD KARNAS

The pedestrian bridge at Hell's Gate gives an impressive
view of the Fraser River flowing below.
JOHN ELK III/GETTY IMAGES

7

RIVERS IN RUINS

I once stopped at a place called Hell's Gate. Here the Fraser River squeezes through an especially narrow passage—only 115 feet (35 meters) wide. The water rampages and roars like an angry beast on its way downstream. As I watched the rushing water, it was hard to imagine that adult salmon could swim up through it. Yet this was the route taken by the sockeye salmon that I swam with in the Stellako River (which I mentioned in the introduction to this book).

The rivers and streams that salmon return to are as varied as the thousands of different salmon populations. They rely on their freshwater habitat to bring the next generation into the world. But many rivers and streams are failing salmon. Why? We humans demand a lot from rivers and streams, and in making those demands, we've caused a fair bit of habitat loss and damage.

A SHADY DEAL

Salmon need streams with cold, clear, strongly flowing water. They need beds of clean gravel—not gravel filled with silt or other sediments. Their young need side channels and pools along the river margins to hide from predators. And they need food—invertebrates that creep along the river bottom and invertebrates that fall into the water from overhanging vegetation.

In the early days of agriculture, forestry, mining and town building, people didn't think about the consequences of cutting all the riparian (streamside) vegetation to clear land right to the edges of streams. But without tree canopies shading the water, it warms up. Without roots holding the banks in place, soil crumbles into the stream. Without overhanging branches and trees to fall in from the edges, the stream loses its hidey-holes and its rainfall of bugs.

As well as cutting down the riparian vegetation, we've drained wetlands, cut rivers off from their *floodplains* and in some places even straightened rivers into concrete-lined canals. We've blasted riverbeds with water from high-pressure hoses to mine metals, and built dams and other barriers to extract water or generate power. We've polluted river water with agricultural runoff and with industrial and urban waste. Pollution affects how juvenile salmon grow, how many eggs an adult female produces and even the ability of a mature adult to find its birth stream.

If rivers are polluted or don't have the right types of habitat, fewer river creatures will live there. This includes not only fish but also insects, crayfish and snails—the food for fish and other animals. Everything is connected!

Top: Dylan Parliament uses a minnow trap to survey juvenile fish in Hastings Creek, BC. MARIA HUDSPITH AND DEB PARLIAMENT

Bottom: Many cities paint fish on the road or use metal medallions to remind residents not to dump garbage or chemicals into storm drains. NANCY NEHRING/GETTY IMAGES

The waterfall coming out of this culvert makes it tricky—or even impossible—for a juvenile salmon to swim farther upstream to habitats with good food and shelter. SARAH HAGGERTY

Sarah Haggerty spends lots of time working outdoors. KIRSTEN UNDERWOOD

"WE'RE HAMMERING [SALMON], BUT WE CAN CHANGE THINGS. NATURE RESPONDS QUICKLY IF WE ALLOW IT TO."
—SARAH HAGGERTY

JUMPING IN

A lot of roads that cross streams use metal tubes called culverts to let water keep flowing while the road runs over top. But many culverts act like crazy water slides with too-fast water. Over time this strong flow washes out the streambed, leaving the culvert dangling above the stream. Fish have a tough time jumping into these culverts and then swimming up through the rushing water.

Working for Maine Audubon, Sarah Haggerty coordinates a program to improve stream crossings. Hundreds of culverts and other crossings are fixed every year, but Maine alone has about 30,000 crossings. "We still have a lot of work to do!" Sarah says. "But Maine has the last rivers with wild Atlantic salmon south of Canada, so we have a huge responsibility."

River-restoration projects can be huge and expensive. Here a large dam has been removed, letting the river return to its original path.
JOEL ROGERS/GETTY IMAGES

REVIVING RIVERS

Projects are underway around the world to restore river habitat for salmon. It won't be possible to return some rivers—especially large ones flowing through urban centers—to completely natural conditions. But restoring even parts of a river's health can make a difference.

In Europe the Rhine River flows along the border between Germany and France and then through the Netherlands. The river's watershed lies in seven different countries and has more than 50 million people living in it. The Rhine was a polluted river, and a lot of its natural habitat had been destroyed. Atlantic salmon, which once returned to the Rhine in the hundreds of thousands, were gone by the 1950s.

In 1986 a fire broke out in a warehouse storing pesticides and herbicides, and in the efforts to put out the fire, a lot of these chemicals ended up in the Rhine River. Millions of fish and other animals died—even eels, which are fairly tolerant of water pollution. This event prompted the countries along the Rhine to work together to improve water quality and river habitat for fish. Their goal was to have Atlantic salmon and other *migratory* fish returning to the river by 2000. And they did exactly that! By 1995 salmon were migrating into the Upper Rhine, and in 2015 more than 700 salmon returned to the river.

Since the original Rhine salmon had died out in the 1950s, biologists used hatchery salmon to restart the Rhine population. The hatchery salmon came from rivers in France, Ireland, Scotland and Sweden.

Many other rivers are being revived in similar ways. In England salmon once again swim in the River Thames, and in Maine they return to the Penobscot River.

Lina Azeez paddles a canoe with traps for catching and identifying fish species in the Fraser River's side channels and sloughs.
MIKE PEARSON

JUMPING IN

When Lina Azeez looks at the Fraser River in British Columbia's Lower Mainland region, she thinks about what's happening in the river's side channels and sloughs. She pictures juvenile salmon—fish about the length of your finger—hunting, hiding and growing on their journey to the sea.

As Vancouver and surrounding areas expanded, people built dikes and floodgates along the river to protect communities and farmland from floods. At the same time, they blocked off many of the places where juvenile salmon like to hang out! In the lower Fraser River, salmon can't access about 900 miles (1,448 kilometers) of side channels, sloughs and streams.

"Lots of the flood infrastructure is old and needs to be upgraded," Lina says. "So it's the perfect time to do the work in a fish-friendly way." She and others at Watershed Watch Salmon Society are promoting green methods of flood control, such as reconnecting the river with its side channels and creating wetlands to absorb floodwaters. "We need to give the river room to flood, and do it safely."

> "SALMON ARE INCREDIBLY BEAUTIFUL AND RESILIENT CREATURES. THEY CAN SURVIVE SO MANY CHALLENGES."
> —LINA AZEEZ

Many dams, like this one on the River Elan in Wales, are beautiful structures, but fish can't jump over them. Only about one-third of the world's longest rivers still flow freely, without being blocked by dams.
FFOTO KEITH MORRIS ABER/GETTY IMAGES

A salmon leaps from one pool to the next in this fish ladder. These structures allow fish to get to the top of a dam or waterfall or around another barrier.
BAXTERNATOR/GETTY IMAGES

THE DAMMED

People have been using the power of moving water for thousands of years. By the 1800s, efficient water wheels called *water turbines* had been invented, making it possible to generate hydropower—literally power (electricity) from water. The most efficient way to create a lot of hydropower is to build a dam across a river that has a large drop in elevation. The dam holds back water, storing it in an artificial lake called a *reservoir* until it's needed. Then water is released to fall through the inside of the dam. The falling water spins turbines, which produce power. The taller the dam, the more power can be generated.

Hydropower stations have dramatic impacts on rivers and river life, making hydropower the third H of human activities that threaten salmon. Salmon struggle with uneven water flow, warmer water, lost habitat and difficult passage up and down a river. Dams block spawners' path upstream unless some kind of fish passage is built. Fish ladders help fish get above a small dam, but they aren't practical at very large dams.

Some dams have water-filled fish elevators to move fish over them, and one of the newest methods is the salmon cannon—a long, flexible tube that "shoots" a fish over a dam. The official name of the machine is the Whooshh Passage Portal. Sounds like a wild ride!

Other dams don't have any fish passage at all. In the Columbia River watershed—which covers parts of Oregon, Washington, Idaho, Montana and British Columbia—dams block fish from getting to about 55 percent of the spawning or rearing habitat they used in the past.

Dams are also a problem for juvenile fish traveling downstream to the ocean. Going over a dam and through a turbine is risky. Some fish die, and those that survive are often stunned by the time they come out the other end. This makes them easy pickings for birds and bigger fish. Some dams have bypass channels so that juveniles can swim safely downstream. Others collect salmon fry in water tanks, and trucks drive them around the dam.

One time, in the 1970s, dam operators in the Columbia watershed loaded juvenile fish into airplanes. The airplanes dropped these "flying" fish into the river below the dam. Ouch. (It didn't work very well either.)

Out of the way! This salmon is on a mission as it leaps up a fish ladder.
DEB PERRY/GETTY IMAGES

Main: The white line to the right of the Cle Elum Dam, WA, is the flexible tube of a salmon cannon.

Inset: A salmon whooshes through the flexible tube.
WHOOSHH INNOVATIONS

JUMPING IN

In 1998 Craig Orr co-founded Watershed Watch Salmon Society, an organization that tackles many of the problems facing Pacific salmon—habitat loss, overfishing, too little water in rivers, fish farms and climate change.

For one project, Craig and Watershed Watch discovered that many hydropower operations in British Columbia were using more water than they were allowed to. So Craig got to work on one of the affected rivers, the Coquitlam River. He helped negotiate and write a water-use plan, an agreement saying who can use a river's water, how much they can use and when they can use it. Slowly things improved for the Coquitlam River. It now has more water flowing in it, which has produced more salmon.

For more than 20 years, Craig has worked to restore water flows and salmon runs on the Coquitlam River. In July 2020 he tweeted this:

Craig Orr
@CraigOrr_

Some good salmon news! The first sockeye of the year returned yesterday to the Coquitlam River. Zero last year. Epic struggle to repair the damage caused by BC's oldest hydroelectric dam continues. Kwikwetlem/Coquitlam literally means #redfishuptheriver. Historically early run.

9:12 PM · Jul 7, 2020 · Twitter for Android

> **"[IN THE COQUITLAM RIVER] THERE WASN'T ENOUGH WATER FOR FISH."**
> —CRAIG ORR

Craig Orr with a steelhead trout before he lets it go. Steelhead trout are closely related to Pacific salmon. CRAIG ORR

TAKING DAMS DOWN

Dam-removal projects are underway on several salmon rivers (or former salmon rivers) in both Europe and North America. In France, the Sélune River used to have Atlantic salmon, but two dams built in the 1910s and 1920s for hydropower blocked fish passage, and the salmon disappeared. Both dams are now being removed to open up 56 miles (90 kilometers) of the river. The World Wide Fund for Nature estimates that 3,500 dams have been taken down across Europe, giving migratory fish access to thousands of miles of rivers and streams.

In the state of Maine, a project that took seven years to complete has opened up nearly 2,000 miles (3,218 kilometers) of the Penobscot River and its tributaries. Two dams were taken down, and a third one got a bypass channel so that Atlantic salmon and other migratory fish can swim upstream to all their original habitat. On the West Coast of North America, two dams were removed from the Elwha River in Washington State, and there are plans underway to do the same on the Klamath River in California. More than 1,700 dams have been taken down over the last 10 years in the United States.

Projects to remove large dams such as these are expensive and take a long time, but many people see value in opening up fish habitat and allowing rivers to return to more natural water flows.

The Glines Canyon Dam came down in a massive dam-removal project that started in 2011. The dam was built in 1927 on the Elwha River, WA.
COURTESY OF THE NATIONAL PARK SERVICE

Peace of Salmon. Ray Troll drew this image for a poster for Salmonfest, a music festival held in Ninilchik, AK, that celebrates the sustainable harvest of salmon. Ray says, "It depicts sockeye salmon in their various life stages, from eggs to spawning adult and death, an eternal cycle that can sustain the runs—and us—if we know how to interact responsibly with this magnificent resource. I'm proud of my hippie heritage, hence the peace sign, and everything just looks cooler with flames. The flames also help to stress the urgency of the situation we're in today." Ray drew the image with pen and ink on paper, and artist Memo Jauregui did the digital coloring. © RAY TROLL, 2018, TROLLART.COM

8

LIFE UNDER THE OCEAN WAVE

In the last chapter, you read about some of the ways people have altered freshwater habitat for salmon. What about ocean habitat? Has it been changed too? The simple answer is yes. Some of the biggest effects on ocean habitat are happening as a result of climate change.

IN HOT WATER

Ocean water around the world is heating up. On average, the ocean surface is about 1°F (0.56°C) warmer now than in 1880. Of course, ocean water isn't the same temperature everywhere, and it's not warming at the same rate everywhere. The ocean is warmer at the surface than at depth, and it's warmer closer to the equator than farther north. There are also various water currents that make some areas warmer and others cooler. All these variabilities make it tricky to find out how warming water affects marine creatures.

Trash floating in the ocean and littering shorelines is a threat to all marine creatures. Joining a shoreline cleanup is a great way to help make a difference.
TAYLOR JONES-ARASON

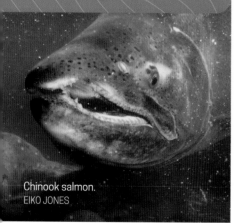

Chinook salmon.
EIKO JONES

Here are some of the challenges salmon face in a warmer ocean:

- **Missing meals**: In the ocean, salmon eat zooplankton and smaller fish, but some of these prey are becoming harder to find. The prey themselves are affected by changes in water temperature, making them less abundant or forcing them to move elsewhere in the ocean (north, south, east, west, deeper, shallower).

- **Eating junk food**: Some prey are becoming less nutritious. For example, Atlantic salmon eat a small fish called capelin. Over the past 40 years, individual capelin in the northwest Atlantic Ocean have become smaller and contain fewer fats. To get a satisfying meal, salmon have to hunt for and eat more capelin, which uses more energy. They may need to eat other prey, often also of poor quality. Overall, the salmon grow slower and are less healthy.

- **Being on the menu**: Changing water temperature can change life for salmon's predators too. If, say, the number or range of porbeagle sharks, bluefin tunas and other predators changes, then they might eat even more Atlantic salmon than they already do.

- **Getting sick**: Diseases and parasites are another can of worms (ahem) in warming ocean waters. Fish may be exposed to new illnesses, or because they're less physically fit, they may be more susceptible to getting sick. Warm water temperature can also interfere with a salmon's *immune system*.

Main: Skil Jaadaa *Vanessa Zahner* examines the contents of a fish's stomach through a microscope.
KRISTINE HO/UBC INSTITUTE FOR THE OCEANS AND FISHERIES

Inset: These critters are copepods, each one about the length of a sesame seed. They look a little mushed up because they've come out of a salmon's stomach!
SKIL JAADAA *VANESSA ZAHNER*

> "[SALMON] HAVE ALL THESE PRESSURES ON THEM, BUT THEY'RE STILL GOING. THEY'RE FLEXIBLE. THEY WILL DO WELL IF WE GIVE THEM THE OPPORTUNITY."
>
> —SKIL JAADAA
> *VANESSA ZAHNER*

JUMPING IN

When salmon smolts enter the sea, they feast on tiny animals called *copepods*, on crab and barnacle larvae, on arrow worms and even on little jellyfish. How do we know what such small fish are eating? We look inside their stomachs, of course!

Skil Jaadaa *Vanessa Zahner*, a graduate student at the University of British Columbia in Vancouver, gets samples of young pink and chum salmon, opens up their stomachs and examines the contents through a microscope. She says that sometimes she can tell exactly what the fish ate. Other times, the contents are all mushy. Eeew! She also finds bits of plastic inside some stomachs, a reminder of all the garbage in the oceans.

Salmon have always been part of Vanessa's life. "Being from the Haida Nation, growing up on Haida Gwaii, the ocean is everything," she says. She considers salmon a relative to give back to, a relative to help. One of her ways of helping salmon is to study their feeding behaviors—what they eat, how much they eat and when they eat.

JUMPING IN

In the mid-1980s, about 10 million Atlantic salmon swam in the oceans and spawned in European and eastern North American rivers. Even that is probably far fewer salmon than there were centuries ago. Today, in the 2020s, there are only 2 to 3 million Atlantic salmon. Do some quick math. How many salmon have disappeared in the last 40 years? About 2 million each decade, so 1 million every five years. That's 200,000 salmon every single year!

The Atlantic Salmon Trust, with Mark Bilsby at its helm, is searching for clues about how these salmon went missing.

For one project, they captured juvenile salmon in a stream and tagged them with tiny tracking devices. Then they followed the fish for 125 miles (201 kilometers) on their journey to the sea. To their great surprise, Mark says, "half of these juveniles went missing before they ever made it out of fresh water."

The Atlantic Salmon Trust and its partners have joined forces as the Missing Salmon Alliance. "The salmon are telling us there's something wrong with their rivers and ocean," Mark says. "We have to take action!"

"THE BIGGEST THREAT SALMON FACE IS APATHY. THERE ISN'T A LIMITLESS SUPPLY [OF SALMON] IN THE OCEAN. WE CANNOT TAKE THEM FOR GRANTED."
—MARK BILSBY

Main: A trap helps with the job of counting salmon smolts as they migrate along the River Oykel in Scotland.
ATLANTIC SALMON TRUST

Inset: Mark Bilsby.
STEVEN RENNIE/ATLANTIC SALMON TRUST

RUNNING OUT OF GAS

Warm water dissolves or holds less oxygen than cooler water. So with climate change warming up the ocean, seawater today holds less oxygen than it did several decades ago. What does less oxygen mean for marine creatures? The same as it does for us! All animals need oxygen to live, whether they live on land or in water. Some species—like jellyfish—tolerate lower oxygen, but other animals, including salmon, aren't so happy.

Oxygen affects where animals live in the water, how many prey are available and how nutritious the prey are. Fish will change their behavior to get to places with more oxygen. This might be an advantage if they go to areas with more prey to eat, or it may backfire if they end up in a place with more predators.

Many coastlines have an extra problem with low oxygen. Urban waste, agricultural fertilizers and *aquaculture* waste can add lots of nutrients to the water. These nutrients encourage algae to grow out of control. When the algae die, bacteria consume them and at the same time use up a lot of the oxygen. Some coastal areas have "dead zones" with no oxygen left at all. Fish and other animals are forced to move elsewhere—if they're able to.

WHEN LIFE GIVES YOU LEMONS

Climate change is making the ocean more acidic. Seawater is 25 percent more acidic today than it was at the beginning of the Industrial Revolution in the late 1700s—just 250 years ago. This change in ocean acidity, called *ocean acidification,* has happened so quickly that marine creatures haven't had much time to adapt. Shellfish have an especially hard time as water gets more acidic, because the acidity "steals" an ingredient they need to make their shells.

For fish, the more acidic water makes their bodies work harder. The acidity upsets the balance of chemicals in their blood and cells, so fish have to use up energy to get rid of the extra acid. This leaves them with less energy for finding food, avoiding predators and growing bigger and stronger. Ocean acidification may also affect their brains. One study of coho salmon is investigating whether juveniles respond differently to smells—an important part of a salmon's ability to migrate back to its birth river.

The nooks and shelves purposely built into this seawall give algae and invertebrates more places on which to attach and grow. More of these creatures means more food for fish like salmon. CITY OF SEATTLE, WASHINGTON

Scientists measure a liquid as acid or alkaline using the pH scale. The lower the pH value, the higher the acidity of the liquid. Seawater is slightly alkaline, similar to our blood. Seawater 250 years ago had a pH of 8.2. Today seawater is about 25 percent more acidic, with a pH of 8.1. No, this percent change is not a mistake! A small change on the pH scale equals a very big change in acidity. BLUERINGMEDIA/SHUTTERSTOCK.COM

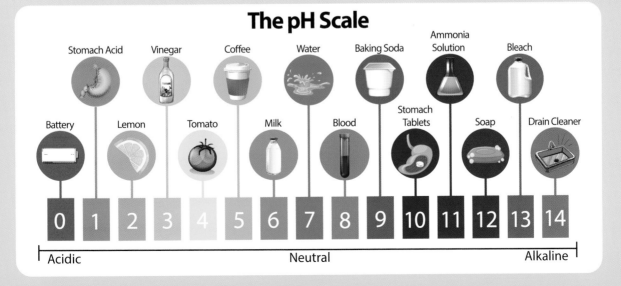

The pH Scale

Stomach Acid · Vinegar · Coffee · Water · Baking Soda · Ammonia Solution · Bleach

Battery · Lemon · Tomato · Milk · Blood · Stomach Tablets · Soap · Drain Cleaner

0 1 2 3 4 5 6 7 8 9 10 11 12 13 14

Acidic · Neutral · Alkaline

Tuktoyaktuk in the Northwest Territories lies near the mouth of the Mackenzie River, where Pacific salmon species are turning up more and more frequently.
PIERRE LONGNUS/GETTY IMAGES

Salmon is on the menu for this sea lion.
SANTIPARP WATTANAPORN/SHUTTERSTOCK

GO WILD

Sea lions and seals are clever creatures. Many have discovered salmon feasts at the base of dams or fish ladders in large rivers like the Willamette and Columbia. To save the salmon, wildlife managers tried to scare the sea lions with noisemakers and rubber bullets. No luck. Then they tried trapping the animals and dropping them off hundreds of miles away. Within a few days, the very same sea lions came back. Starting in 2020, the United States gave the okay for some of these sea lions to be killed. Unfortunately, animal culls often don't solve the problem.

OPENING NEW DOORS

In the past a few Pacific salmon—usually pink and chum—strayed into Arctic waters, but very few. Now "Arctic salmon" are becoming a thing, with more Pacific salmon turning up in the Canadian Arctic. Even the occasional Atlantic salmon is caught. In northern Canada, the Arctic Salmon Project collects salmon from fishers. In 2019 fishers caught nearly 2,500 salmon across the Canadian Arctic. That's more salmon in a single year than in all the previous 18 years.

With water warming up, more salmon may be straying north to get into cooler water. Habitat in the Arctic that previously was inaccessible or didn't have the right conditions might also now be more salmon friendly. Salmon aren't the only species moving into new territory, a response called *range shift*. More than 12,000 species around the planet have shifted their range—and those are just the ones scientists have documented.

Some species move into new territory and start causing mayhem. These are "wanted" animals—like a criminal is wanted. Biologists call them *invasive species*. For example, European green crabs, originally found in Europe and North Africa, were carried first to eastern North America by boats and then to California in packing materials. From these spots, the crab larvae have moved through coastal waters along both eastern and western North America. As adults, these crabs greedily feed on shellfish and native crab species, and they disrupt meadows of eelgrass used by juvenile fish, including salmon.

Invasive species typically tolerate a wide range of environmental conditions. European green crabs are especially good at dealing with changes in temperature, so warming seawater may help them move even farther into new territories, where they will disturb more habitats and harm more native organisms.

Residents of northern Canada help scientists track salmon in the Arctic by turning in the heads of fish they catch, or even entire fish, to the Arctic Salmon Project.
ARCTIC SALMON PROJECT, FISHERIES AND OCEANS CANADA

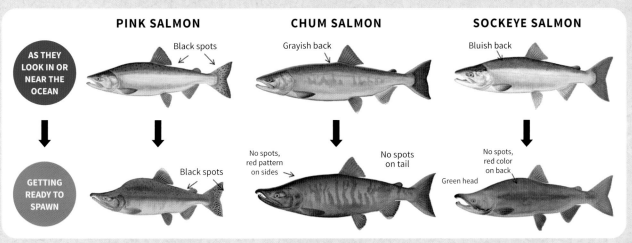

ARCTIC SALMON
We will be accepting UNLIMITED salmon heads and 10 whole fish per community.
Contact your local HTO/HTC or RRC office for information on how to obtain your reward.

PINK SALMON

CHUM SALMON

SOCKEYE SALMON

AS THEY LOOK IN OR NEAR THE OCEAN

Black spots

Grayish back

Bluish back

GETTING READY TO SPAWN

Black spots

No spots, red pattern on sides

No spots on tail

No spots, red color on back

Green head

FREEZE the salmon. You must provide catch date to receive a gift card.
$25 per salmon head or $50 per whole fish

A young student holds a bucket of salmon fry hatched in a tank in their classroom.
CHPSTOCK/SHUTTERSTOCK.COM

9

MEDDLING WITH NATURE

When my kids were in elementary school, I loved going on their class field trips. My favorite was to Goldstream River in late May or early June. There the teacher lugged a heavy plastic bucket with dozens of salmon fry to the edge of the river. The fry had grown from eggs in a tank in the classroom. Each student scooped river water into a small plastic bag and lined up to receive two or three fry. Then they trotted to the river's edge and gently—for the most part—released their captives. "Goodbye, little fishy," some of them called.

On these field trips, I saw the excitement of young children who had watched an organism hatch and were now delivering it to a "forever home" to grow up. But where did these salmon eggs come from?

A BRIGHT IDEA?

In Europe, in the 1400s, people got a new idea. Why not hatch fish artificially, taking the job of fertilizing and incubating fish eggs away from nature and doing it in tanks of water? It didn't catch on right away, but by the mid-1800s people were hatching trout and salmon in places called, not surprisingly, *hatcheries*. In a salmon hatchery, eggs and hatchlings—the alevins—stay in tanks, and when they grow to the size of fry or parr, they are released into the wild. The fish grow up at sea, and thanks to their homing instinct, come back as adults to spawn.

As the Industrial Revolution took off in the 1800s, people were certain they could control nature and make it produce what they wanted. Salmon hatcheries opened in France, Scotland and England, and also in the United States and Canada. Later Japan, Russia and other countries built hatcheries. It seemed like the ideal solution to fix dwindling fish populations. People had destroyed habitat and overfished, but that was okay, because they could just make more fish. Simple, right?

Workers at a hatchery in Utah remove eggs from a female kokanee salmon. Notice how small the fish is. She's a mature adult, but because kokanee live their entire life in fresh water, they never grow as big as the oceangoing sockeye salmon. The scientific name for both kokanee and sockeye salmon is *Oncorhynchus nerka*.
JOHNNY ADOLPHSON/SHUTTERSTOCK.COM

Two-day-old Atlantic salmon at a hatchery in New York State. The salmon will later be released into streams that flow to Lake Ontario. This lake once had the world's largest population of freshwater (landlocked) Atlantic salmon, but they were all gone by the late 1890s.
MARISA LUBECK/US GEOLOGICAL SURVEY

Kentaro Morita gets ready for a snorkel survey of fish in this stream.
MARI KUROKI

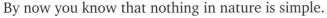

JUMPING IN

The Toyohira River flows through Sapporo, a city of 2 million people on the west coast of Hokkaido, Japan's large northern island. Like many rivers in big cities, it was polluted, dammed and degraded. The number of chum and cherry salmon returning to the river dwindled. So in the 1980s, the city built hatcheries to restock the river with salmon fry.

But in the past 10 years, concern for wild fish has been growing. The genes from hatchery-born fish seem to be getting into and tainting the wild populations. So in 2014 Kentaro Morita and other volunteers started the Sapporo Wild Salmon Project to promote wild salmon conservation. So far they have decreased the number of hatchery fish released each year and improved natural spawning habitats.

> "EVERY ANIMAL SHOULD
> BE ABLE TO LIVE ITS
> LIFE WITHOUT HUMAN
> INTERVENTION."
> —KENTARO MORITA

By now you know that nothing in nature is simple.

Many of the hatcheries didn't work. Despite hatching thousands of eggs and pumping the resulting juvenile fish into rivers, the number of adult spawners rarely increased. All the destroyed habitat was a problem, because once out in the rivers and ocean, hatchery fish need habitat just as much as wild fish do. But many people didn't see it that way. They persisted in their belief that an industrial solution to declining fish populations was the right solution.

Today hatcheries grow and release both Atlantic and Pacific salmon. A lot of people have very strong opinions about hatcheries and whether they're useful or harmful.

A teacher scoops salmon fry to place in a student's waiting plastic bag. The child will then release the small fish into a nearby stream.
ROWENA RAE

TO HATCH...

People in favor of hatcheries believe these operations help keep salmon populations alive. The Penobscot River in Maine has a salmon hatchery program. The river has also had a lot of work done to improve the habitat, including removing multiple dams to give salmon access to much more of the river. In 2020 around 1,500 adult salmon returned to the Penobscot—six times more fish than just six years earlier. That's an impressive increase. But was it thanks to the hatchery program or to the restored habitat? The answer depends on how you view hatcheries.

Advocates also believe that hatcheries are contributing to lucrative commercial salmon fisheries through *ocean ranching*. The hatchery-born fish are released to graze and grow in the ocean. When they're caught as adults and sold in a store, they are often labeled as "wild-caught." With a hatchery origin, they aren't wild fish, but they're harvested from the wild.

These Atlantic salmon fry don't seem too sure about leaving the safety of their bucket to live in a wide, open river.
ALANNA SYLIBOY

...OR NOT TO HATCH

People who are against hatcheries see these operations as the fourth H of human activities that threaten salmon. A big concern with hatcheries is their potential to taint the *gene pool* of wild salmon. When hatcheries began operating, nobody realized that different rivers have genetically distinct populations of salmon. But they do. Over thousands of generations, the salmon in River X have adapted to conditions in their river, while the salmon in River Y have adapted in a different way to *their* river. The genetic adaptations in hatchery fish are different again.

Inevitably, some hatchery fish spawn with wild fish, and their hatchery-adapted genes enter the wild population. Therefore, say many biologists, the wild population loses some of its *genetic fitness*—the population has fewer "good" genes to pass on to the next generation of salmon. For an individual fish, this means not having some of the adaptations needed to survive in the wild.

Hatcheries also raise other concerns. For every species in an ecosystem, there is a *carrying capacity*—the number of individuals the ecosystem can support. But salmon ecosystems may not have enough habitat and food for all the hatchery salmon as well as the wild ones. Hatchery fish compete with wild salmon for food, and they sometimes even eat smaller wild salmon.

Also, when commercial fishers are harvesting hatchery salmon in the ocean, they will inevitably catch wild salmon that are swimming alongside the hatchery fish. This contributes to overfishing the wild populations.

The debate about hatcheries—whether they're good or bad—goes on. And while it does, the countries rimming both the North Pacific and the North Atlantic collectively hatch and release billions of salmon every year.

A worker at a fish hatchery throws a chinook salmon down a sorting tube.
PHOTOGRAPHY BY ADRI/GETTY IMAGES

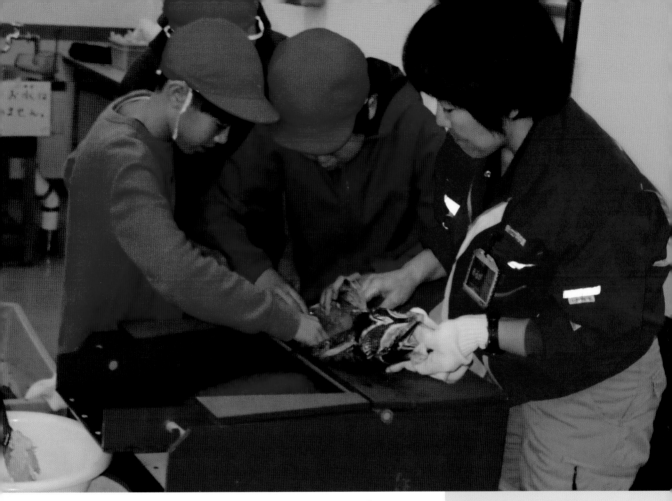

On a class visit to the Sapporo Salmon Museum in Japan, students scoop eggs out of a female salmon for a hatchery program.
SAPPORO SALMON MUSEUM

SALMON IN SCHOOLS

Like my kids' school, many schools have programs for students to keep a tank of salmon (or trout) eggs in their classroom and later release the fry into a local stream. How different is this from large hatcheries incubating eggs and releasing millions of fry? There's a difference of scale— tens or hundreds of eggs in classrooms versus millions in hatcheries. But in the minds of some people, there is no real difference. A hatchery salmon is an artificially raised fish, and it poses risks for wild salmon. To other people, these programs have value for helping students learn about salmon and ecosystems and taking students into nature.

At this Norwegian salmon farm, the rims of 12 circular cages float peacefully on the surface of the water. Contained in the underwater nets are tens of thousands of Atlantic salmon.
ANDREY ARMYAGOV/DREAMSTIME.COM

10

CAGED CREATURES

On a visit to Scotland years ago, I walked along a cliff path on the Isle of Skye and came to the crest of a hill. Looking into the sheltered bay below, I saw 10 large circles floating in two neat rows of five. I hadn't a clue what they were, but I liked their symmetry. I later asked about the circles and learned they formed a salmon farm. It was like a field of cattle, except in the ocean. I just couldn't see the occupants—the thousands of salmon swimming in net cages below the water surface.

FARMING FISH

Salmon are a recent addition to aquaculture—which is culturing, or growing, aquatic animals and plants for people to eat. This watery form of agriculture likely began about 4,000 years ago in China, with carp grown in ponds. In Egypt, people began farming a fish called tilapia, and the ancient Greeks and Romans farmed eels. Indigenous Peoples on the West Coast of North America also managed shellfish "gardens" starting thousands of years ago.

A market stall sells fresh steaks of Atlantic salmon farmed in Norway.
CHRISTIAN THOMAS/GETTY IMAGES

Salmon farming began in Norway in the 1960s and soon spread elsewhere in Europe, to Canada and the United States (both eastern and western coasts) and even to Australia, New Zealand and Chile—in the southern hemisphere where salmon are not native.

Salmon farms differ from salmon hatcheries. Farms produce adult-size fish and never intentionally release them into the wild. Salmon farms artificially breed salmon—just like hatcheries do—but once the fish are big enough to adapt to seawater, salmon farmers transfer them to floating ocean cages. The cages are made of netting, allowing seawater to flow in and out. Farmers throw food pellets to the caged fish, which grow for one or two years before being caught, processed and sent to market.

A few farms grow Pacific salmon species, but the overwhelming majority of farmed salmon are Atlantic salmon.

THE TIP OF THE ICEBERG

Net cages are deceptive. From the surface they don't look like much. A farm can have 10 to 30 net cages anchored as close as 325 feet (99 meters) offshore. Each cage has a square or circular rim at the ocean surface and netting that extends 30 to 50 feet (9 to 15 meters) deep. Each cage can "house" 15,000 to 30,000 fish.

A whale shark, the largest fish species in the world, swims past a net full of forage fish, which are among the smallest fish in the ocean.
MATHIEU MEUR/STOCKTREK IMAGES/GETTY IMAGES

The ideal site for a net cage is in a fjord or near a river's mouth, where water flows into the sea. These locations typically have good water currents to maintain temperature and oxygen and also remove the nutrient-rich waste pooped out by the thousands of caged fish. Even with water currents, this large load of nutrients can cause unwanted algae to grow in the water and change the types of shellfish and other organisms living on the seafloor.

FEEDING CARNIVORES

How many deer would it take to feed a field full of cougars? We don't farm cougars, so we don't know. Raising carnivorous livestock on land is difficult to imagine. But that doesn't stop us at sea.

Salmon are carnivores, which means they eat other animals—insects, shrimp, other invertebrates, small fish. Salmon growing in a net cage eat pellets made from a combination of fish meal, fish oil and plant-based ingredients such as soy, corn or wheat. The fish meal and oil come from small wild fish called *forage fish*, which include anchovies, herring and menhaden. But many populations of these forage fish are in trouble from overfishing. Forage fish could go directly to feed people, but most are funneled into the fish- and animal-feed markets. It's an inefficient way to produce food, and it's unsustainable for ocean food webs.

In the 1980s fish meal and oil from forage fish made up about three-quarters of the ingredients in fish-feed pellets. Today they constitute about one-quarter or less. Feed manufacturers have been finding alternatives. Companies are researching insects, such as black soldier fly larvae, and feather meal (made by pressure-cooking poultry feathers) as high-protein ingredients for feed pellets.

A worker shovels feed pellets to hungry Atlantic salmon at a farm in Maine. Can you see the pellets sinking into the water?
KEVIN FLEMING/GETTY IMAGES

A big storm wrecked this salmon farm in Puget Sound in 2017, letting thousands of Atlantic salmon escape into Pacific waters. WILD FISH CONSERVANCY

GO WILD

Most salmon in the southern hemisphere live in fish farms, but some have *naturalized*. They successfully spawn in streams, go out to sea and migrate back to streams, just like salmon in their native range. Chinook originally from California now live in the Patagonian region of Chile and the South Island of New Zealand. They are descendants of salmon deliberately stocked in southern streams or of fish-farm escapees. The problem is, these salmon are *exotic species* in southern hemisphere streams, and they are using habitat and eating food that should be going to native fish species.

JAILBREAK

Fish in net cages are like prisoners in a jail. If they get a chance to escape, they will. Sometimes storms damage the nets or seals rip holes in them. In a case in Washington State, in 2017, a salmon farm failed to clean the nets regularly. Seaweed and thousands of mussels and other invertebrates grew on them, adding over 100 tons (91 metric tons) of weight. Eventually the nets collapsed, and more than 250,000 Atlantic salmon escaped into Puget Sound.

All over the world, hundreds of thousands of farmed salmon have escaped. When farmed Atlantic salmon escape in coastal areas of the Atlantic Ocean, there's a risk of the farmed fish spawning with wild fish and affecting the genetic fitness of wild populations. In the Pacific, escaped Atlantic salmon can't mate with wild Pacific salmon to produce future generations, because they're different species. But escapees can compete with wild salmon for food and habitat, and they can spread diseases and parasites.

Skyla Tomine and her brother, Weston, go salmon fishing with their dad whenever they get the chance. The fish Skyla's holding is a chinook salmon.
DYLAN TOMINE

JUMPING IN

When Skyla Tomine was eight, she landed her first salmon—a silvery coho weighing six pounds (2.7 kilograms). A few years later, her class incubated salmon eggs in a tank. When it was time to release the fry into the local river, Skyla and some friends sat out of the activity in protest. Their teacher misunderstood. "She thought we were scared the fish would bite us," Skyla says. Yeah, right. Not a kid who could land a six-pound fish—with teeth—on her own. She was protesting the origin of the classroom fry. Skyla thinks hatchery fish have no place in the wild.

As a teen, Skyla participates in other protests. A few years ago she joined a rally against net-cage salmon farms in the coastal waters near her home on Bainbridge Island, Washington. The protest paid off. Legislation went before the state government, and in 2018 lawmakers voted against Atlantic salmon farming. New farms aren't allowed to start up, and existing ones must stop growing Atlantic salmon by 2022.

"[JOINING A PROTEST] FELT POWERFUL. PEOPLE CAME FROM ALL OVER."
—SKYLA TOMINE

Protesters in Tofino, BC, take to the street with a message for the salmon-farming industry and the governments that oversee the farms.
DOUGLAS LUDWIG FOR THE NUUCHAHNULTH SALMON ALLIANCE

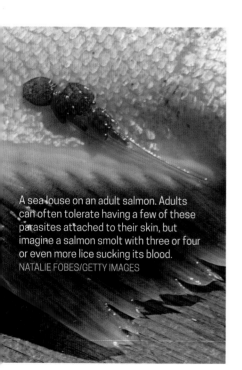

A sea louse on an adult salmon. Adults can often tolerate having a few of these parasites attached to their skin, but imagine a salmon smolt with three or four or even more lice sucking its blood.
NATALIE FOBES/GETTY IMAGES

HAVING LICE ISN'T NICE

I had head lice as a kid, and it was no fun. These little *crustaceans* are parasites—they feed on a host animal so they can reproduce. In the ocean, there are different crustaceans called sea lice, and some live on salmon. Before salmon farming, wild fish had a few sea lice on them, but usually not many. With the start of salmon farming, a lice dining buffet opened. Thousands of salmon confined in net cages make perfect feeding and breeding grounds for sea lice.

Sea lice larvae swim in the water until they find a fish and anchor to its scales. The larvae then molt into adults and feed on the fish's skin and blood while looking for a mate. Lice can eat through their host fish's skin, creating sores open right down to the bones. The wounds can be severe enough to kill a salmon.

When a lice-infested salmon farm is near a wild salmon migration route, the result can be disastrous. As long as a salmon is the right species, sea lice aren't picky about their host's origin or life. Farmed, wild, adult, juvenile— any type is fine. A juvenile salmon with many lice doesn't have much of a chance to survive.

To remove sea lice and prevent outbreaks, salmon farmers have tried killing the lice with chemicals—but this isn't a great solution, because the chemicals can be harmful to other crustaceans too. For instance, lobster fishers in eastern Canada report catching fewer lobsters near salmon farms that use chemical treatments. Another solution is to control the lice by adding "cleaner" fish, such as wrasse, to the net cages to eat lice off the salmon.

SICK SALMON

Farmed salmon also get sick with diseases caused by viruses and bacteria. A cage of sick salmon threatens migrating wild fish, and it also raises concerns about the overuse of antibiotic medications. The more antibiotics that are used, the more chances there are of bacteria evolving ways to stay alive and keep growing. When this happens, the bacteria are called *antibiotic-resistant*—the antibiotic no longer kills them. Antibiotic-resistant bacteria are a serious problem for animals, including people, throughout the world.

Emiliano Di Cicco, in the dark jacket, examines a juvenile chinook salmon.
GIDEON MORDECAI

> "WE HAVE ALMOST NO KNOWLEDGE OF THE ROLE OF DISEASE IN WILD FISH."
> —EMILIANO DI CICCO

JUMPING IN

As a university student in Matelica, Italy, Emiliano Di Cicco had a "fish room" with 800 gallons (3,028 liters) of water in fish tanks—enough to fill about 20 standard-sized bathtubs! Emiliano became a vet and specialized in fish pathology (the study of diseases that affect fish). He and a team of people are now trying to find out if infectious diseases—those caused by viruses, bacteria, parasites or funguses—are one of the reasons that wild Pacific salmon are in trouble.

It's tricky work! Observing a disease outbreak in the wild is tough, especially in the ocean, since sick fish are weak and usually get eaten before their illness shows up. Emiliano says looking for sick fish in the ocean is like stumbling around without a flashlight inside a huge black box. Since 90 percent or more of all salmon die in their first year of life in the ocean, Emiliano wants to study juveniles, but it's especially hard to follow small fish in the ocean. "With juvenile salmon, the black box is even more black," says Emiliano.

So far Emiliano and his colleagues have found at least 50 infectious agents (bacteria, viruses, fungi and parasites) in 30,000 salmon. Next, they plan to figure out when these agents cause disease in wild salmon, and how farmed and hatchery salmon are involved.

Ocean Farm 1 being towed 3 miles (4.8 kilometers) out to sea, off the coast of Norway. When it's in the right spot, the huge cage will be lowered and anchored so that only the top yellow rim and the white command center remain above water. The cage can house about 1.5 million Atlantic salmon at a time.
SALMAR

CHANGING PLACES

Many biologists, environmentalists and citizens—myself included—would be happy for the salmon-farming industry to simply stop and close up shop. But that's unlikely to happen. Salmon farming provides more than 130,000 jobs around the world and makes a lot of money—$15 billion US in 2018.

So are there ways to fix some of the problems or make them less harmful? Yes!

Marine pollution, escaped fish and sea-lice infestations could all be prevented by pulling net cages out of the ocean and instead growing salmon in closed tanks on land. It takes a lot of energy to keep large on-land tanks of water at the right temperature, and all that water needs to go through sewage treatment. For these reasons the salmon-farming industry has resisted moving their farms to land. But recently some companies in Europe, North America and elsewhere have started taking the plunge.

Another idea is to take salmon farms away from coastlines and far out to sea. A Norwegian company is experimenting with a submersible system in the open ocean. Offshore farms wouldn't pollute coastal areas, and they would reduce the chance of migrating wild salmon swimming nearby. Escapee fish could still be a problem, though.

Raising salmon in water tanks on land is costly, but it solves some of the environmental problems associated with ocean net cages.
MARISA LUBECK/US GEOLOGICAL SURVEY

For a project with Watershed Watch Salmon Society, Elise Carelse measures a juvenile coho salmon captured from a creek in Chilliwack, BC.
WATERSHED WATCH SALMON SOCIETY

CONCLUSION
A FUTURE FOR SALMON?

As I wrote this book, I spoke with a lot of people who work with or think about salmon every day. They all told me similar things.

They worry about the many, many, *many* impacts humans have on salmon and their environments. They also worry about the kind of world we will have if salmon and their diverse ecosystems disappear completely.

They also have hope. They see passion in the people working to make habitat, water quality and other parts of ecosystems better for salmon. They see the growing awareness of nature among people from all sorts of backgrounds. They see energy in youth who want and deserve a healthy home planet to live on and share with the world's creatures.

None of us can see the future, but we can picture how we'd like it to look. I would like it to look like the Stellako River—the place I described in the introduction to this book. I would like a future in which salmon thrive, and with them, the whole ecosystem, including us humans.

How do you want the future to look for yourself and your friends and family? For nature? For rivers and oceans? For wild salmon?

A school of sockeye salmon.
EIKO JONES

From picturing the future, we need to jump up and help create that future. Here are some ideas for where you can put your energy to make a future that includes wild salmon.

Learn about the rivers, streams and lakes in your watershed. What's your nearest water-body? Do salmon live there? What other fish and animals live there? Are they healthy or in trouble? Think about what you could do to lessen your impact on your watershed. Commit to using less water. Walk or bike more often. Plant native trees.

Look for a river-guardian or streamkeeper group to join. These groups love new volunteers to help with streamside planting, fish counts, shoreline cleanups and other projects. Get out and get your hands dirty for fish!

Celebrate World Fish Migration Day. This celebration happens every second year, in October. The next one is in October 2022.

Use seafood guides to help choose which fish to buy. Several organizations track information about fish populations and fishing practices. California's Monterey Bay Aquarium has a Seafood Watch program that labels seafood as "best choices," "good alternatives" or "avoid." Others to check out are Ocean Wise and Environmental Defense Fund's Seafood Selector.

Know the source of the salmon that you and your family buy. Good fish vendors and chefs know where the fish they sell comes from. Ask them! Ask which salmon species it is and whether it's farmed or wild. If it's farmed, ask more questions about the type of farm and where it's located. If they don't know, consider buying salmon elsewhere or ordering a different meal.

Tread as lightly as you can on salmon habitats. Even if you don't live near the coast or near a salmon river, you can make a difference. For instance, we contribute to climate change, which warms up river and ocean water. So walk, bike and use transit as much as possible. And we contribute to plastic pollution, a lot of which ends up in freshwater and ocean environments. So buy less stuff—ask yourself, Do I really need this? Say "no, thanks" to single-use plastic items. Every effort counts, and the more of us who take actions, the better the overall effect.

Spread the word to classmates, friends and family. Tell them what you've learned about salmon and aquatic environments from reading this book. Expand your research by reading online about current events related to salmon. Explain how you're making a difference for salmon, and challenge them to join you.

Take and post photos on social media. Use the camera in your pocket to take photos of nature—places related to salmon or not—and share them on social media. Share what you love about the natural world and also your concerns.

Spend time outdoors, and think about your connection not only to salmon but to all of nature. We all—me included—need to become more aware of our place on this planet. We are just one species, one part of nature, one cog in the complex ecosystems on planet Earth. We must understand and appreciate our place so that we have a reason to protect it.

Tim Elder is all set to count juvenile coho and other fish near the wood structures his team placed into West Fork Evans Creek, OR. "As soon as you put wood into a stream," Tim says, "small fish just show up in droves."
BRIAN KELLY

JUMPING IN

Tim Elder started his career as a salmon biologist on the Columbia River, but after several years he was ready to turn his attention to smaller rivers. He now works for Wild Salmon Center and spends his time planning and doing habitat restoration on coho salmon rivers in southwest Oregon. He and his crew add large wood to streams, make cold-water refuges, remove small barriers and plant streamside vegetation.

On the Columbia River, he witnessed the immense dams and their negative effects on habitat and fish. Those dams supply electricity to millions of people in the Pacific Northwest and will remain on that river for the foreseeable future. But southwest Oregon's rivers have fewer and smaller dams, and many of the habitat problems are fixable. For Tim, it's all about tackling the things that he can do something about.

"OUR ENVIRONMENT WON'T GET BETTER WITH JUST A FEW PEOPLE DOING ALL THE WORK. IT CHANGES WHEN EVERYONE DOES A LITTLE TO HELP. THERE ARE THINGS WE CAN ALL DO EVERY DAY."

—TIM ELDER

GLOSSARY

adaptations—the ways in which organisms adjust to living in a new environment or to living with changes in their current environment

alevin—a newly hatched salmon that is living off its yolk sac

algae—aquatic organisms that use photosynthesis, like plants do. Some algae are microscopic and some, including seaweeds, are visible to the naked eye.

anadromy—the lifestyle of fish that hatch in fresh water, migrate to the ocean to grow into adults and return to fresh water to spawn the next generation

antibiotic-resistant—of bacteria: surviving exposure to medicines that previously would have killed them

aquaculture—growing aquatic animals and plants as food

aquatic—relating to water; growing in or living in water

bycatch—the fish and other marine organisms caught unintentionally in commercial fishing

carnivorous—of an animal: feeding mainly on other animals

carrying capacity—the number of individuals in an animal or plant population that an ecosystem can support with the available food, habitat and other resources

common ancestor—a species that two or more other species are descended from over evolutionary time

crustaceans—a group of invertebrate animals with two pairs of antennae and more than three pairs of legs, such as crabs, lobsters, shrimp, lice and fleas

ecosystem engineers—organisms that play a large role in creating, changing, maintaining or destroying a habitat they live in

ecosystems—the communities in which the plants, animals and nonliving things (rocks, soil, water) of a particular place exist together

escapement—the number of adult fish that escape capture and other dangers and return to their birth stream to spawn

estuary—the place where river water mixes with tidal ocean water

exotic species—a plant or animal species that is not native to the habitat in which it's living; also called an alien species (see *invasive species*)

food webs—the feeding relationships among species in an ecosystem

floodplains—the land on either side of a river that floods during times of high water flow

forage fish—small fish that are prey for predators such as larger fish, birds and mammals

fry—a young salmon that has absorbed its yolk sac and has emerged from the gravel on the riverbed—it is in the next life stage after alevin

gene pool—all the different genes found in a species or a population

genes—the basic units that make up the set of instructions in cells for making proteins, which are the "building blocks" of life

genetic fitness—the ability of an organism to reproduce successfully. Genetic fitness depends on how well the organism is adapted to its environment.

genetically distinct—having variations in the genes so that one group of organisms has different adaptations from other groups of organisms in the same species

genus—a classification of organisms that share certain traits because they are closely related

habitat—the place where an organism lives

hatchery—a facility where the eggs of fish or other animals are hatched under artificial conditions

hydropower—electricity generated by the power of moving water

immune system—the network of parts in the body that recognizes germs and defends against them

imprinting—rapid learning in an organism's early life that influences the organism's behavior later in life

indicator species—an animal or plant species that tells us something important about the health of the environment it lives in

Industrial Revolution—a period in history that started in the mid-1700s in Britain with the invention of steam engines and changed society from an agricultural to a manufacturing economy

invasive species—a plant or animal species that harms the ecosystem it lives in. Most invasive species are also not native to the habitat where they're living (see *exotic species*).

invertebrates—animals without a backbone, such as snails, crabs, shellfish and insects

kelt—a salmon that has spawned but not yet swum back out to sea

kype—hooked jaw of some male salmon when they're ready to breed

larvae—the immature stage of insects and other organisms, like frogs, that go through a transformation to become adults

magnetic field—the area where a magnetic material (for example, iron or nickel) exerts a pulling (magnetic) force. Earth's magnetic field is charged by molten iron and nickel in the planet's outer core. The magnetic field extends into space, and some organisms can detect and use it for navigation and migration.

migratory—of an animal: moving from one place to another with the seasons or in different life stages

milt—the fluid that contains sperm in a male fish

mouth—the place where a river flows into another body of water

naturalized—of a plant or animal: established and living in a place where it is not native

ocean acidification—the process of ocean water becoming more acidic as the carbon dioxide the ocean absorbs reacts with the seawater to produce acid. It is caused primarily by excess carbon dioxide in the atmosphere.

ocean ranching—a way of growing fish by releasing hatchery-born fish to swim freely in the ocean and grow into adults for harvest

oxbows—U-shaped bends in a river

parr—a young salmon that has camouflage markings on its body and still lives in fresh water. Parr is the stage between fry and smolt.

poached—caught or killed illegally

population—organisms of the same species that live in the same geographic area at the same time and can reproduce with one another

predators—animals that prey on other animals for food

range shift—a change in the geographical area occupied by a species, usually because of climate change

redd—a hollow or nest made by a female salmon in the gravel of a riverbed to lay her eggs in

refugia—areas where plant and animal species can survive harsh environmental conditions, such as glaciation

reservoir—an artificial lake, usually made by building a dam across a river to hold back water

riparian—occurring alongside rivers and streams

roe—fish eggs

salmon run—a salmon population as it migrates upriver from the sea to spawn

sloughs—marshy side channels of a river or bay

smolt—a young salmon as it migrates from fresh water out to sea

spawning—the laying of eggs by a female fish which are then fertilized by a male fish

terrestrial—related to the land or referring to an organism that lives on land (as opposed to in water)

watershed—the entire land area on which precipitation falls and then drains into a particular body of water

water turbine—a type of water wheel that converts the power of water into electrical current (electricity)

zooplankton—small animals that are suspended in water and drift in water currents. Some zooplankton can swim weakly.

RESOURCES

PRINT

Boochever, Annie. *Bristol Bay Summer*. (Fiction.) Portland, OR: Alaska Northwest Books, 2014.

Cone, Molly. *Come Back, Salmon: How a Group of Dedicated Kids Adopted Pigeon Creek and Brought It Back to Life*. Friday Harbor, WA: Sierra Club Books for Children, 2001.

Gyetxw, Hetxw'ms (Brett David Huson). *The Sockeye Mother*. Winnipeg, MB: Highwater Press, 2017.

Joe, Donna. *Salmon Boy: A Legend of the Sechelt People*. Gibsons, BC: Nightwood Editions, 2001.

Peelen, Lori, and Robert Elofson. *I Am the Elwha*. Nanaimo, BC: Strong Nations Publishing, 2020.

Rae, Rowena. *Upstream, Downstream: Exploring Watershed Connections*. Victoria, BC: Orca Book Publishers, 2021.

ONLINE

Atlantic Salmon Federation: asf.ca

Atlantic Salmon Trust: atlanticsalmontrust.org

Environmental Defense Fund's Seafood Selector: seafood.edf.org

International Year of the Salmon: yearofthesalmon.org

Living Oceans Society: livingoceans.org

Marine Stewardship Council: msc.org

Monterey Bay Aquarium's Seafood Watch: seafoodwatch.org/seafood-recommendations

Ocean Wise seafood guide: seafood.ocean.org/seafood

Pacific Salmon Foundation: psf.ca

Salmon & Trout Conservation: salmon-trout.org

Watershed Watch Salmon Society: watershedwatch.ca

Wild Fish Conservancy: wildfishconservancy.org

Wild Salmon Center: wildsalmoncenter.org

World Fish Migration Foundation: worldfishmigrationfoundation.com/portfolio-item/world-fish-migration-day

FILMS/VIDEOS

Patagonia Films. *Artifishal: The Road to Extinction Is Paved with Good Intentions*. patagonia.ca/stories/artifishal

Patagonia Films. *DamNation: The Problem with Hydropower*. patagonia.ca/video-79847.html

Project Media Conservation through Education. *To the Journey's End: The Life Cycle of the Atlantic Salmon*. project-media.co.uk/work

Sitka Conservation Society. *The Salmon Forest*. sitkawild.org/the_salmon_forest

For a complete list of references, visit the page for this book at orcabook.com.

ACKNOWLEDGMENTS

I have many people to thank for helping me learn about salmon, both as I wrote this book and long before I began it.

For the indelible experience of swimming with sockeye in the Stellako River, I thank my co-swimmers: my sister, Elspeth Rae; my brother-in-law, Matthew Carter; and my then-soon-to-be-husband and now ex, but still good friend, Andrew Wilson—the biologist who organized the float.

For telling me two decades ago that I should be writing about salmon, I thank Ann Finkbeiner, my mentor in the Writing Seminars at Johns Hopkins University.

When I was embarking on the research for this book, my friend Deana Machin and International Year of the Salmon director Mark Saunders were wonderful about introducing me to interesting and knowledgeable people, many of whom I interviewed to profile in the book.

I'm very grateful to the 22 people I interviewed—named in the pages of the book—for their time spent "Zooming" with me and answering my many questions. The following people assisted me with additional information or photos: Andrew Wilson, Daniel Schindler, Dylan Tomine, Eiko Jones, Emma Helverson, Jessica Walsh, John Marriott, John Reynolds, Karen Dunmall, Kelly-Ann Turkington, Kurtis Hayne, Leslie Budden, Lindsay Wrapson, Lisa Simonsen, Lori Howk, Maria Hudspith, Melissa Kim, Nick Hawkins, Ray Troll, Sandra Gradek, Sue Pollard, Tim Williams, Tom Moffatt and Vianna Murday.

Thank you to the people who graciously agreed to review and comment on the manuscript: Fred Whoriskey, a marine biologist at Dalhousie University; Deana Machin, an independent fisheries management and policy researcher from Syilx Okanagan Nation; Christy Wilson, a salmon biologist and educator; Aaron Hill and Anna Kemp, both with Watershed Watch Salmon Society. They all made suggestions that have improved the manuscript. However, any errors in the text are mine.

Many, many thanks to Carolyn Combs, writer friend and critique partner, for giving me super feedback on the manuscript and for always making time to encourage me and help me strengthen my writing. Thanks, too, to friend and editing partner Merrie-Ellen Wilcox for "Onchy"—a salmon cushion that has become my read-aloud buddy.

At Orca Book Publishers, I'm deeply grateful to Kirstie Hudson, my editor, whose patience I sorely tried while I wrote this manuscript. Kirstie's editing first helped me trim my behemoth of a manuscript to a more manageable length and then helped me express my ideas much more smoothly. Thank you to Vivian Sinclair for her careful copyediting, Mark Grill for searching out photos and handling permissions, Dahlia Yuen for her beautiful layout and all the others in the fabulous team at Orca who have helped this book see the light of day. I also acknowledge the British Columbia Arts Council for funding.

For encouragement of my writing habit, I thank my father, Angus Rae, who passed away while I was writing this book. Even in his final days, he asked for news of my writing progress. I thank my mother, Ann Skidmore, for her constant support and also for so frequently feeding me and my children; my sister, Elspeth Rae, for patience as I let this project overtake her and my fiction writing project; my walking friends, Sharilynn Wardrop and Mariana Vitek, for thoughtful and interesting conversations; my partner, Travis Commandeur, for unfailing understanding when I disappear into my writing and also for pulling me back out to see the big picture over a glass of red wine. And my greatest thanks to my children, Genevieve and Madeleine, for loving that their mother is a writer and for not just accepting but embracing our sometimes scattered lifestyle.

INDEX

*Page numbers in **bold** indicate an image caption.*

ROWENA RAE worked as a biologist specializing in aquatic ecosystems and fisheries in Canada and New Zealand before becoming a freelance writer, editor and children's author. She is the author of *Rachel Carson and Ecology for Kids*, as well as *Chemical World* and *Upstream, Downstream* in the Orca Footprints line. Rowena writes both fiction and nonfiction from her home in Victoria, British Columbia.